A Digital Framework for Industry 4.0

Ana Landeta Echeberria

A Digital Framework for Industry 4.0

Managing Strategy

Ana Landeta Echeberria
Universidad a Distancia de Madrid
Madrid, Spain

ISBN 978-3-030-60048-8   ISBN 978-3-030-60049-5   (eBook)
https://doi.org/10.1007/978-3-030-60049-5

This Palgrave Macmillan imprint is published by the registered company Springer Nature Switzerland AG.
The registered company address is: Gewerbestrasse 11, 6330 Cham, Switzerland

I dedicate this book to Edorta Landeta Echeberria and José Antonio Álvarez López, for sharing with me their characteristic sound reason and for their unconditional support at all times.

FOREWORD

When Dr. Ana Landeta suggested to this writer that I might write a foreword to her book *A Digital Framework for Industry 4.0 Managing Strategy*, I didn't hesitate for a second. Firstly, because I thought it was a magnificent book. Secondly, because not only is its subject matter important but because it's a book about and concerning a vitally important, immediate question, the Fourth Industrial Revolution. It is a book that fills a gap or, to put it more accurately, a deep schism among so much doxogrpahic literature on the topic that offers opinion and little or nothing in the way of the nature of the revolution or the scientific and pragmatic contribution that this book from Dr. Landeta provides.

Having said that, the first thing we have to ask ourselves is for whom is this book intended? The response is two-fold. It is aimed directly at entrepreneurs and managers at all levels of institutions, companies and business who have already or are yet to assume the digital transformation, because it involves them greatly. But this book should also be read by politicians as it concerns them too, on the one hand to "refine" their worldview and take stock of the world in which they operate in order to judiciously exercise their functions. Indirectly, it's a book aimed at the each and every one of the inhabitants of this Earth, as this is a revolution that will affect each and every one of us. In summary, it affects everyone, concerns some and implicates a specific few.

On reading that, someone might ask, what's the difference between someone it concerns and someone it implicates? The best way to answer that is through the analogy of breakfast. Bacon and eggs might be the cornerstone of a traditional breakfast. That concerns the hen, who has to lay eggs but for whom it's not a matter of life or death. The pig, meanwhile, is implicated, as it has to be sacrificed in order to obtain the bacon.

The second question is what is the book about and how does it deal with the issued. In terms of the content of the book, the answer to that is found conveniently in the title. As for the how, we must state the following. Of the book's five chapters, the first three serve to prepare us for tackling the challenge of digital transition. Over the last two years, a reasonable, suitable and complete and above all effective solution has been developed for the challenge of this transition from the Third Industrial Revolution to the Fourth Industrial Revolution. In doing so, the author, sometimes tacitly but more often implicitly, follows Rudyard Kipling's rule of the six honest serving men. In his marvellous poem *The Elephant's Child*, Kipling wrote, "I keep Six honest serving men/ (They taught me all I knew);/ Their names are What and Why and When/ And How and Where and Who."

More specifically, in Chap. 1, "The Industrial Internet and Potentially Economically Disruptive Technologies", not only is the Fourth Industrial Revolution defined, but its origins and its principal characteristics are also considered. It also looks at the segments of the current transformation, the challenges involved and the opportunities it generates. It ends with the technologies that involve and, or especially concern Artificial Intelligence with significant potential to direct and advance that disruption and its economic and social impact, as well as its challenges and implications. The definition itself is no small matter; as Nobel laureate André Lwoff wrote in Biological Order, "Defining is one of the methods of discovery. It is, as a matter of fact, an excellent heuristic method as it forces one to consent the essential nature of a category or a phenomenon into a formula; a formula that contains that which it must contain and excludes that which it must exclude, For that reason it is useful to forge a good definition as this exercise obliges one to critically consider all the terms or aspects of the question." The definition offered by Dr. Landeta meets Lwoff's requirements to the letter.

In Chap. 2, "The New Economy and New Business Models", the author offers, from the outset, a sharp criticism of the oft-repeated and false assertion that leadership cost and differentiation should be considered equally effective strategies. She goes on to put forward four scenarios to consider the subject from a more suitable, realistic perspective than that of Porter for example.

Having just cited Lwoff, she approaches a definition of the "new economy", establishing, clearly and succinctly, the principal elements of transformation and the theoretical perspective. She goes on to emphasise the peculiar aspects of the digital information economy such as minimal marginal costs, their network of externalities and barriers, facilitators of, and those reluctant to embrace, change in the business model. She ends by looking at the current successful digital business models, their origins and the general outline of their development, underlining the best practices identified.

Chapter 3, "Digital Transformation Business Landscape", presents the benefits of digital transformation, and two perspectives on it. The four dimensions of the strategies of that transformation are considered and the procedural aspects of those strategies are argued. There follows an explanation of how to integrate digital transformation within companies, institutions and businesses, signalling important challenges and strategic paths to achieve effective transformation.

Chapter 4, "Digital Transformation Implementation Plan", presents the roadmap for the implementation of digital transformation: the phases of development and integration and the metrics of monitoring and control, especially in terms of pay-off, ROI and the KPIs to be taken into account.

Finally, Chap. 5, "Digital Transformation Strategy Framework", presents the book's principal and original contribution. It constitutes an effective, working framework (even a novice in the area would be capable of implementing it) for digital transformation that's efficient (using the bare minimum of resources of any kind), necessary and adaptable to any kind of company, institution, business or area of activity. The working framework included patterns, focuses, steps and metrics to monitor and control the entire process.

With the structure explained, allow me to share some of my impression of the chapters. Sir Francis Bacon, Lord Verulam and 1st Viscount Saint Albans, in his *Novum Organum* of 1620, said that there were two types of writings: The "luminiferous" and the "fruitful." The first three chapters of Dr. Landeta's book are luminiferous in the sense that they shed light on and illuminate the scenario and environment for the proposed framework and of the state of the art thereof. She does so, to follow the Verulian terminology, through the faculty or art of sound judgement.

For their part, Chap. 4 and, in particular, Chap. 5 are fruitful in that they provide the procedure to follow to produce the digital transformation results sought.

The book falls under the informational genre and its structure is very specific: the data (values to take a variable), which are parsed. The news (meaning that an intelligent being providing data) constitute what commonly, in a clear case of synecdoche, is called information and they are present semantically. Pragmatic knowledge that serves to resolve problems and make better decisions. While the first three chapters present the data and the news, the final two chapters concern knowledge.

Summarising, Dr. Landeta's framework is certainly a roadmap for any organisation to gradually reach adaptation of the Fourth Industrial Revolution. But it's much more, as it is an authentic GPS that stops those using it from straying too far from the correct, optimal path or reaching digital transformation. And all without a mathematical formula.

Stephen Hawking, in the acknowledgements of his famous work *A Brief History of Time*, wrote: "Someone told me that each equation I included in the book would halve the sales. So I decided not to include any. At the end, however, I did include one equation, Einstein's famous $E = mc^2$. I hope that this doesn't scare off half my potential readers." Hawking was right and his book was a huge success.

For this writer, if there were one equation to be included in this book it would be Aiken's version; $S = mc^2$ or Success = motivation commitment squared, in a little known article from 1986. The success of any activity, in this case digital transformation, is a function of motivation and commitment. For the conductor of the Los Angeles Philarmonic Orchestra, Essa Peca Solonen, motivation is "driving the energy and passion of each individual toward the freedom to do what they do of their own wishes, not because it is imposed." "Only motivated people and enthusiasts can carry out quality processes and simultaneously be satisfied and gratified by the effort invested." I have previously written that commitment can be reached in different ways, including the following: offering opportunities to compare different perspectives of the same question. Providing interactive feedback of information, principally in the form of knowledge from a working group. Setting challenges that require intellectual effort. Without a doubt, the development of the digital transformation framework offers all those possibilities in abundance.

With the right criteria, the author avoids where possible "Hoffman's Illusion" or the magic of mathematics or "scientism." Nevertheless she does use maths in a way that is very attractive assimilable for anyone with a normal level of intelligence. The diagrams and graphic representations of the methods, techniques and procedures used are an example of that. It's a great success.

And two final points before I finish. One, to emphasise the total adaptability of the proposed framework. Rev. Charles Lutwidge Dodgson, better known by his pen name Lewis Carroll, in Christmas 1871, published *Through The Looking Glass And What Alice Found There*, containing this dialogue between Alice and the Queen of Hearts. The Queen says, "Now, here, you see, it take all the running you can see, it takes all running you can do, to keep in the same place. If you want to get somewhere else, you must run at least twice as fast as that!" And in an intensely dynamic world where the only constant is change, such as the world of the Fourth Industrial Revolution, only an adaptable framework can survive and advance. What is proposed in his book is completely adaptable.

Two, this book is not the fruit of Dr. Landeta's mental elucubrations, the result of the previous work and experience of her doctoral thesis. Mark Twain once said person that had taken a bull by the tail knows five or six things more than someone who hasn't. Undoubtedly, the author has not only caught the Fourth Industrial Revolution by the tail, but in the style of the Portuguese *forçados*, has grabbed it by the horns too; straight on and with no concessions.

And so, dear reader, buy Dr. Landeta's book and read it. It's not a purchase; it's an investment, and offers epistemic profits and high economic return. And to make things interesting, why not take a pen and paper and assign each of the proposals in the book to Kipling's six honest serving men? Just so!

Spain   Pazos Sierra

PREFACE

Dear readers,

This book is the result of the work I have conducted over several years. It is an adaptation of my doctoral thesis *A Digital Transformation Strategy Model for Companies within the Industry 4.0 Framework*, defended in October 2018.

It is a research work adapted for the general public using, I hope, a more informative discursive approach. I have always believed in the importance of transferring the results of academic work to the business world and to society.

When I began studying the Fourth Industrial Revolution phenomenon I was fascinated and began to think about the challenges we face. About how much the world around us is going to change and the extent of the general transformation we face—social political, commercial and personal—in the present and in the near future.

This book is a response to the rapid changes in the capacity and performance of information and communication technologies and their potential, as we seek to develop effective strategies within the framework of full digital transformation and business competitiveness. The impacts of the latest disruptive technologies have yet to be fully explored and understood, with widespread adoption of new innovations within the Fourth Industrial Revolution scenario.

The themes of the book are perhaps more relevant now than ever, with the digitalization of the business fabric becoming an imperative as the Covid-19 crisis has forced many businesses to accelerate their digitalization plans.

If the results I present in this book are put into practice or used by an entrepreneur, as they see fit, in even one case, then I'll be satisfied.

I hope you find it a useful and gratifying read.

Madrid, Spain   Ana Landeta Echeberria
August 2020

ACKNOWLEDGEMENTS

I have had two great influences in my career: one in the academic world and one in the professional sphere.

Firstly, there is my academic mentor, Professor of Artificial Intelligence, Professor Juan Pazos Sierra.

Thanks to Dr Pazos Sierra I obtained my PhD and continue learning every day, devoting myself to those who show an interest as I try to continue to make inroads on this exciting scientific journey.

Thank you for always being there.

In the professional sphere, there is Roque de las Heras Miguel, honorary president and founder of the CEF-UDIMA Education Group to which I have belonged for 20 years.

From Roque I have learned the value of perseverance, enterprise and hard work and tackling things with enthusiasm, humility and common sense.

Thank you for believing in me, Roque.

CONTENTS

LIST OF FIGURES

LIST OF TABLES

Introduction

This book is motivated by the rapid changes in the capability and performance of information and communication technologies (ICT) and their potential in order to develop effective strategies in the framework of full digital transformation at different levels; political, social, economic, urban and industrial production transformations and, moreover, in terms of business competitiveness. The impact of the latest disruptive technologies, however, is still not well explored and understood, with the intensive adoption of different innovations within the Fourth Industrial Revolution scenario.

In a moment of reflection about the changes that the economy and digital societies introduce and of management of the fears and the uncertainties in which any modern society subsists by the innovation and the social control of the change trying to anticipate the future in order to plan it we are witnessing an intense and accelerated process of transformations derived from the application of information and communication technologies with profound repercussions on the economy, work and society.

In this sense, it is necessary to analyse the impact of the current era of changes on the labour market, both because of its implications in terms of how many and what jobs will require an economy in constant and accelerated transformation, as well as its consequences on the quality of employment as a guarantor of social cohesion. In the economic sphere there is a renewed interest in the study of digitisation in relation to economic growth and employment.

This process of accelerated transition on a global scale within the economy and society tends to be identified as the fourth industrial revolution or more popularly known as Industrial Internet or Industry 4.0: a fact that together with the constant evolution of technology promotes digital transformation.

Digital transformation is a cultural and strategic change that affects the organizational model of the company, its processes and its technology.

Digital transformation is a journey that can be broken down into different phases but that, in short, is the process of change that is necessary to allow a company to compete in the market with "native digital" companies that place the customer at the centre of the organization and always seek to simplify their work in order to be able to digitalize.

In the macroeconomic context, the industrial revolution, consisting of incorporating new technologies (cloud, cyber-physical and sensor system among many others) into industry, constitutes a new industrial journey that is already being undertaken by many countries.

Digital transformation constitutes a challenge for the worldwide industry but it also offers an opportunity to improve its competitive position.

For this reason, the main contribution of this book is the construction of a strategic digital transformation operational framework, which is necessary and adaptable to any type of company and sector of activity.

The book tries to fill the gap in the strategic digital transformation operational framework. Its main objectives are to

- Examine the relationships between digital transformation and Industry 4.0 with business landscape, and
- Contribute to a better understanding of the challenge for the worldwide industry and to provide businesses with an opportunity to improve their competitive position.

Therefore, the strategic framework suggested includes the patterns, actions, approaches and several measures that are detailed below, and fully explained in Chap. 5.

- A pattern for preparing an Internal Training Plan adapted to digital strategy.
- An association of digital elements in the training plan based on the financial profitability model.

- An alignment of the competence framework with the development plan and the axes of the digital strategy and the company's internal training plan.
- A model proposed for the internal training plan adapted to the company's digital strategy within the framework of Industry 4.0.
- A practical approach for the integration of new mechanisms in instructional design associated with the programmes inherent in the Internal Training Plan adapted to the digital strategy.
- A synthetic model to enable companies to prepare digital transformation plans (tool for diagnosing the level of digital maturity and a scorecard tool for the assessment and actions associated with the scope of the optimum degree of digital maturity).
- A Digital Strategic Framework (elements and phases).
- A Digital Transformation Strategy Plan (phases and actions).
- A Digital Strategy's Balanced Scorecard.

CHAPTER 1

The Industrial Internet and the Potentially Economically Disruptive Technologies

This first chapter is based on Industry 4.0 in its entirety; origin, definition of the Fourth Industrial Revolution, its main characteristics, current transformation segments, challenges and opportunities, the presence of companies in worldwide network Industry 4.0, the disruptive technologies with a significant potential to drive economic impact and disruption, implications and challenges for business leaders in this new technological and business landscape.

1 THE INDUSTRIAL INTERNET (INDUSTRY 4.0): CONCEPT AND CONTEXT

Acccording to the findings of an analytical study on 'Industry 4.0' carried out by Policy Department of the European Parliament, the concept of Industry 4.0 (German Federal Ministry of Education and Research, Project of the Future: Industry 4.0) regards it as a series of disruptive innovations in production and leaps in industrial processes resulting in significantly higher productivity. It is viewed as the fourth time such a disruption took place following

1. The First industrial revolution when steam power combined with mechanical production led to the industrialisation of production in the late 1700s.

A. Landeta Echeberria, *A Digital Framework for Industry 4.0*, https://doi.org/10.1007/978-3-030-60049-5_1

2. The Second industrial revolution when electricity and assembly lines resulted in mass production from the mid-1800s onwards.
3. The Third industrial revolution when electronics and IT combined with globalisation greatly accelerated industrialisation since the 1970s.

According to this logic, the fourth industrial revolution links intelligent factories with every part of the production chain and next generation automation that has started to occur since about 2010 (Werner and Shead 2013).

In their view, it is somewhat of an oversimplification to characterise the first and subsequent industrial revolutions in this way, and economic historians will differ as to whether this would be a continuation of the third or the beginning of a fourth industrial revolution. Also, this model does not point out that with each "revolution", national industrial leadership has changed—from England, to Germany and the Continent of Europe, and then the United States. But two key questions to be answered are about the extent to which this would be a "disruptive" technology that changes the rules of the game and leads to a leap in productivity (rather than incremental change), and if so, the extent to which such change can be generalised throughout the economies of Member States (all, some, which, how, etc.) and sectors that can be affected (and to what extent, etc.). Nevertheless, the argument does fit in with the observed evolution of industrial systems away from the Taylorist and Fordist[1] approach that has increasingly characterised production systems since the 1970s.

Although it may be that Artificial Intelligence is the disruptive technology with the greater applicability in the near future.

This is corroborated by the *The One Hundred Year Study on Artificial Intelligence,* launched in the fall of 2014 produced by Stanford University.

AI is a science and a set of computational technologies that are inspired by—but typically operate quite differently from—the ways people use their nervous systems and bodies to sense, learn, reason, and take action. While the rate of progress in AI has been patchy and unpredictable, there have been significant advances since the field's inception 60 years ago. Once a mostly academic area of study, twenty-first century AI enables a

---

[1] Taylorism—the 'scientific management' approach that breaks tasks down into smallest components; Fordism—the approach to standardised mass production pioneered by the Ford motor company.

constellation of mainstream technologies that are having a substantial impact on everyday lives.

Nilsson (2010) has provided a useful definition of AI:

> Artificial intelligence is that activity devoted to making machines intelligent, and intelligence is that quality that enables an entity to function appropriately and with foresight in its environment.

These trends drive the currently "hot" areas of AI research into both fundamental methods and application areas:

- **Large-scale machine learning** concerns the design of learning algorithms, as well as scaling existing algorithms, to work with extremely large data sets.

  Deep learning, a class of learning procedures, has facilitated object recognition in images, video labeling, and activity recognition, and is making significant inroads into other areas of perception, such as audio, speech, and natural language processing.

  Reinforcement learning is a framework that shifts the focus of machine learning from pattern recognition to experience-driven sequential decision-making. It promises to carry AI applications forward toward taking actions in the real world. While largely confined to academia over the past several decades, it is now seeing some practical, real-world successes.
- **Robotics** is currently concerned with how to train a robot to interact with the world around it in generalizable and predictable ways, how to facilitate manipulation of objects in interactive environments, and how to interact with people. Advances in robotics will rely on commensurate advances to improve the reliability and generality of computer vision and other forms of machine perception.
- **Computer vision** is currently the most prominent form of machine perception. It has been the sub-area of AI most transformed by the rise of deep learning. For the first time, computers are able to perform some vision tasks better than people. Much current research is focused on automatic image and video captioning.
- **Natural Language Processing**, often coupled with automatic speech recognition, is quickly becoming a commodity for widely spoken languages with large data sets.

- **Research** is now shifting to develop refined and capable systems that are able to interact with people through dialog, not just react to stylized requests. Great strides have also been made in machine translation among different languages, with more real-time person-to-person exchanges on the near horizon.
- **Collaborative systems research investigates models and algorithms** to help develop autonomous systems that can work collaboratively with other systems and with humans.
- **Crowdsourcing and human computation** research investigates methods to augment computer systems by making automated calls to human expertise to solve problems that computers alone cannot solve well.
- **Algorithmic game theory and computational social** choice draw attention to the economic and social computing dimensions of AI, such as how systems can handle potentially misaligned incentives, including self-interested human participants or firms and the automated AI-based agents representing them.
- **IoT** research is devoted to the idea that a wide array of devices, including appliances, vehicles, buildings, and cameras, can be interconnected to collect and share their abundant sensory information to use for intelligent purposes.
- **Neuromorphic computing** is a set of technologies that seek to mimic biological neural networks to improve the hardware efficiency and robustness of computing systems, often replacing an older emphasis on separate modules for input/output, instruction-processing, and memory.

So that, the Gartner Top 10 Strategic Technology Trends for 2018 elaborated by (Panetta 2017), are based on the following statement.

Artificial Intelligence, immersive experiences, digital twins, event thinking and continuous adaptive security create a foundation for the next generation of digital business models and ecosystems.

"The continuing digital business evolution exploits new digital models to align more closely the physical and digital worlds for employees, partners and customers," says David Cearley, vice president and Gartner Fellow, at Gartner 2017 Symposium/ITxpo in Orlando, Florida. "Technology will be embedded in everything in the digital business of the future".

The evolution of intelligent things, such as collective thinking car swarms, is one of 10 strategic trends with broad industry impact and significant potential for disruption.

As follows, the strategic trends mentioned above in detail:

The Intelligent Digital Mesh

Gartner calls the entwining of people, devices, and content and services the intelligent digital mesh. It's enabled by digital models, business platforms and a rich, intelligent set of services to support digital business.

Intelligent: How AI is seeping into virtually every technology and with a defined, well-scoped focus can allow more dynamic, flexible and potentially autonomous systems.

Digital: Blending the virtual and real worlds to create an immersive digitally enhanced and connected environment.

Mesh: The connections between an expanding set of people, business, devices, content and services to deliver digital outcomes.

Intelligent

Trend No. 1: AI Foundation

The ability to use AI to enhance decision-making, reinvent business models and ecosystems, and remake the customer experience will drive the payoff for digital initiatives through 2025.

Given the steady increase in inquiry calls, it's clear that interest is growing. A recent Gartner survey showed that 59% of organizations are still gathering information to build their AI strategies, while the remainder have already made progress in piloting or adopting AI solutions.

Although using AI correctly will result in a big digital business payoff, the promise (and pitfalls) of general AI where systems magically perform any intellectual task that a human can do and dynamically learn much as humans do is speculative at best. Narrow AI, consisting of highly scoped machine-learning solutions that target a specific task (such as understanding language or driving a vehicle in a controlled environment) with algorithms chosen that are optimized for that task, is where the action is today. "Enterprises should focus on business results enabled by applications that exploit narrow AI technologies and leave general AI to the researchers and science fiction writers", says Cearley.

Trend No. 2: Intelligent Apps and Analytics

Over the next few years every app, application and service will incorporate AI at some level. AI will run unobtrusively in the background of many familiar application categories while giving rise to entirely new ones. AI has become the next major battleground in a wide range of software and service markets, including aspects of ERP. "Challenge your packaged software and service providers to outline how they'll be using AI to add business value in new versions in the form of advanced analytics, intelligent processes and advanced user experiences", notes Cearley.

Intelligent apps also create a new intelligent intermediary layer between people and systems and have the potential to transform the nature of work and the structure of the workplace, as seen in virtual customer assistants and enterprise advisors and assistants.

"Explore intelligent apps as a way of augmenting human activity, and not simply as a way of replacing people", says Cearley. Augmented analytics is a particularly strategic growing area that uses machine learning for automating data preparation, insight discovery and insight sharing for a broad range of business users, operational workers and citizen data scientists.

Trend No. 3: Intelligent Things

Intelligent things use AI and machine learning to interact in a more intelligent way with people and surroundings. Some intelligent things wouldn't exist without AI, but others are existing things (i.e. a camera) that AI makes intelligent (i.e. a smart camera). These things operate semi-autonomously or autonomously in an unsupervised environment for a set amount of time to complete a particular task. Examples include a self-directing vacuum or autonomous farming vehicle. As the technology develops, AI and machine learning will increasingly appear in a variety of objects ranging from smart healthcare equipment to autonomous harvesting robots for farms.

As intelligent things proliferate, expect a shift from stand-alone intelligent things to a swarm of collaborative intelligent things. In this model, multiple devices will work together, either independently or with human input. The leading edge of this area is being used by the military, which is studying the use of drone swarms to attack or defend military targets. It's evident in the consumer world in the opening example showcased at CES, the consumer electronics event.

Digital

Trend No. 4: Digital Twins

A digital twin is a digital representation of a real-world entity or system. In the context of IoT, digital twins are linked to real-world objects and offer information on the state of the counterparts, respond to changes, improve operations and add value. With an estimated 21 billion connected sensors and endpoints by 2020, digital twins will exist for billions of things in the near future. Potentially billions of dollars of savings in maintenance repair and operation (MRO) and optimized IoT asset performance are on the table, says Cearley.

In the short term, digital twins offer help with asset management, but will eventually offer value in operational efficiency and insights into how products are used and how they can be improved.

Outside of the IoT, there is a growing potential to link digital twins to entities that are not simply "things". "Over time, digital representations of virtually every aspect of our world will be connected dynamically with their real-world counterparts and with one another and infused with AI-based capabilities to enable advanced simulation, operation and analysis", says Cearley. "City planners, digital marketers, healthcare professionals and industrial planners will all benefit from this long-term shift to the integrated digital twin world". For example, future models of humans could offer biometric and medical data, and digital twins for entire cities will allow for advanced simulations.

Trend No. 5: Cloud to the Edge

Edge computing describes a computing topology in which information processing and content collection and delivery are placed closer to the sources of this information. Connectivity and latency challenges, bandwidth constraints and greater functionality embedded at the edge favors distributed models. Enterprises should begin using edge design patterns in their infrastructure architectures—particularly for those with significant IoT elements. A good starting point could be using colocation and edge-specific networking capabilities.

While it's common to assume that cloud and edge computing are competing approaches, it's a fundamental misunderstanding of the concepts. Edge computing speaks to a computing topology that places content, computing and processing closer to the user/things or "edge" of the networking. Cloud is a system where technology services are delivered using Internet technologies, but it does not dictate centralized or decentralized service delivering services. When implemented together, cloud is used to create the service-oriented model and edge computing offers a delivery style that allows for executions of disconnected aspects of cloud service.

Trend No. 6: Conversational Platforms

Conversational platforms will drive a paradigm shift in which the burden of translating intent shifts from user to computer. These systems are capable of simple answers (How's the weather?) or more complicated interactions (book a reservation at the Italian restaurant on Parker Ave).

These platforms will continue to evolve to even more complex actions, such as collecting oral testimony from crime witnesses and acting on that information by creating a sketch of the suspect's face based on the testimony. The challenge that conversational platforms face is that users must communicate in a very structured way, and this is often a frustrating experience. A primary differentiator among conversational platforms will be the robustness of their conversational models and the API and event models used to access invoke and orchestrate third-party services to deliver complex outcomes.

Trend No. 7: Immersive Experience

Augmented Reality (AR), Virtual Reality (VR) and mixed reality are changing the way that people perceive and interact with the digital world. Combined with conversational platforms, a fundamental shift in the user experience to an invisible and immersive experience will emerge. Application vendors, system software vendors and development platform vendors will all compete to deliver this model.

Over the next five years the focus will be on mixed reality, which is emerging as the immersive experience of choice, where the user interacts with digital and real-world objects while maintaining a presence in the physical world. Mixed reality exists along a spectrum and includes head-mounted displays (HMD) for AR or VR, as well as smartphone- and tablet-based AR. Given the ubiquity of mobile devices, Apple's release of ARkit and iPhone X, Google's Tango and ARCore, and the availability of cross-platform AR software development kits such as Wikitude, we expect the battles for smartphone-based AR and MR to heat up in 2018.

Mesh

Trend No. 8: Blockchain

Blockchain is a shared, distributed, decentralised and tokenised ledger that removes business friction by being independent of individual applications or participants. It allows untrusted parties to exchange commercial transactions. The technology holds the promise to change industries, and although the conversation often surrounds financial opportunities, blockchain has many potential applications in government, healthcare, content distribution, supply chain and more. However, many blockchain technologies are immature and unproven, and are largely unregulated.

A practical approach to blockchain demands a clear understanding of the business opportunity, the capabilities and limitations of blockchain, the trust architecture and the necessary implementation skills. Before embarking on a distributed-ledger project, ensure your team has the cryptographic skills to understand what is and isn't possible. Identify the integration points with existing infrastructures, and monitor the platform evolution and maturation. Use extreme caution when interacting with vendors, and ensure you are clearly identifying how the term "blockchain" is being used.

Trend No. 9: Event-Driven

Digital businesses rely on the ability to sense and be ready to exploit new digital businessmoments. Business events reflect the discovery of notable states or state changes, such as completion of a purchase order. Some business events or combinations of events constitute business moments—a detected situation that calls for some specific business action. The most consequential business moments are those that have implications for multiple parties, such as separate applications, lines of business or partners.

With the advent of AI, the IoT, and other technologies, business events can be detected more quickly and analysed in greater detail. Enterprises should embrace "event thinking" as part of a digital business strategy. By 2020, event-sourced, real-time situational awareness will be a required characteristic for 80% of digital business solutions, and 80% of new business ecosystems will require support for event processing.

Trend No. 10: Continuous Adaptive Risk and Trust

Digital business creates a complex, evolving security environment. The use of increasingly sophisticated tools increases the threat potential. Continuous adaptive risk and trust assessment (CARTA) allows for real-time, risk and trust-based decision-making with adaptive responses to security-enabled digital business. Traditional security techniques using ownership and control rather than trust will not work in the digital world. Infrastructure and perimeter protection won't ensure accurate detection and can't protect against behind-the-perimeter insider attacks. This requires embracing people-centric security and empowering developers to take responsibility for security measures. Integrating security into your DevOps efforts to deliver a continuous "DevSecOps" process and exploring deception technologies (e.g. adaptive honeypots) to catch bad guys that have penetrated your network are two of the new techniques that should be explored to make CARTA a reality.

As regards the dynamics allegedly having a disruptive potential in the transformation of production encapsulated by the term "Industry 4.0", it is argued by the proponents of the idea that it is now for the first time possible to link previously isolated elements of the production chain via RFID (radio-frequency identification) chips or the so-called mini transponders (Werner and Shead 2013). This means that each product can have digital information embedded into it that can be shared via radio signals as it moves along the production line, and these products can then communicate with each other independent of human interference. The information thus generated can be analysed with big data and cloud computing processes which allows detecting and addressing invisible issues such as machine degradation, component wear, and so on in the factory floor. To the degree that this is done automatically, smart devices are then capable of managing manufacturing operations and optimising them autonomously by adjusting their own parameters as they sense certain properties of an unfinished product. Moreover, these technological improvements make it possible to customise products to a single unit, drawing the consumer into the production process in a form of 'mass customisation' (Kagermann et al. 2013). This, in turn, allows producers to respond swiftly to changing customer demands and market conditions.

The underlying logic of this manufacturing transformation is characterised by:

- Horizontal integration through networks: The networks can be managed in real time—from the moment an order is placed right though to outbound logistics;
- End-to-end digital integration of engineering across the entire value chain ranging from design, inbound logistics to production, marketing, outbound logistics and service to after- sales service; and
- Vertical integration and networked manufacturing systems where the IT systems at levels of sensor, control, production, manufacturing, execution and corporate planning work together and production, production processes and automation will be designed and commissioned virtually in one integrated process and through the collaboration of producers and suppliers. Physical prototypes will become less important (Table 1.1).

1.1   Definition and Development

In accordance to Deloitte in its report "Industry 4.0",[2] the term Industry 4.0 refers to a further developmental stage in the organisation and

---

[2] Cited also, available from https://www.theseus.fi/handle/10024/123113.

Table 1.1 Industry 4.0—SWOT table

Strengths	Weaknesses
• Increased productivity, (resource) efficiency, (global) competitiveness, revenue	• High dependence on resilience of technology and networks: small disruptions can have major impacts
• Growth in high-skilled and well-paid jobs	• Dependence on a range of success factors including standards, coherent framework, labour supply with appropriate skills, investment and R&D
• Improved customer satisfaction—new markets: increased product customisation and product variety	• Costs of development and implementation
• Production flexibility and control	• Potential loss of control over enterprise
	• Semi-skilled unemployment
	• Need to import skilled labour and integrate immigrant communities
Opportunities	**Threats**
• Strengthen Europe's position as a global leader in manufacturing (and other industries)	• Cybersecurity, intellectual property, data privacy
• Develop new lead markets for products and services	• Workers, SMEs, industries, and national economies lacking the awareness and/or means to adapt to Industry 4.0 and who will consequently fall behind
• Counteracting negative EU demographics	• Vulnerability to and volatility of global value chains
• Lower entry barriers for some SMEs to participate in new markets, links to new supply chains	• Adoption of Industry 4.0 by foreign competitors neutralising EU initiatives

Source: European Parliamentary Research Services

management of the entire value chain process involved in manufacturing industry. Another term for this process is the "Fourth Industrial Revolution".

The concept of Industry 4.0 is widely used across Europe, particularly in Germany's manufacturing sector. In the United States and the English-speaking world more generally, some commentators also use the terms the 'Internet of Things', the 'Internet of Everything' or the 'Industrial Internet'.

What all these terms and concepts have in common is the recognition that traditional manufacturing and production methods are in the throes of a Digital Transformation. For some time now, industrial processes have increasingly embraced modern IT, but the most recent trends go beyond simply the automation of production that has, since the early 1970s, been driven by developments in electronics and IT (see Fig. 1.1).

The concept of Industry 4.0 is relatively recent and consists, fundamentally, of the inclusion of digital technologies in industry. Such inclusion will lead to the technological development and dynamic growth of the sector, exponential growth of flexibility of production, in the personalisation of products and in the optimisation of decision-making. In short, it consists of the emergence of new business opportunities.

Digitalisation constitutes a key opportunity to improve competitiveness of Spanish industry in an increasingly globalised and more uncertain market. Along these lines, the European Commission has set an objective, in the framework of European industrial policy, that the contribution of industry to European Gross Domestic Product (GDP) reaches 20% in the

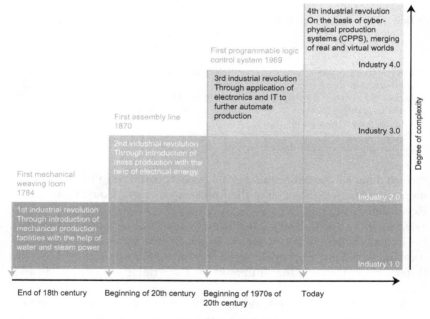

Fig. 1.1 Definition of Industry 4.0. (Source: Author's own, produced from the survey results)

year 2020, turning digitalisation into one of the key drivers of meeting this objective.

In this context, the Ministry of the Economy, Industry and Competitiveness has launched, through the General Secretariat for Industry and Small and Medium-Sized Enterprises, the *Industria Conectada 4.0* strategy, with the aim of driving Digital Transformation in Spanish industry and ensuring its competitiveness. This report is framed within the new strategy of digitalisation of industry and we hope that it becomes a national and international point of reference to better understand this revolution.

The term *Industry 4.0* refers to a stage of additional development in the organisation and its way of managing the entire value chain process involved in the manufacturing industry. Another term for this process is "the fourth industrial revolution".

1.2 Main Characteristics

The following four main characteristics of Industry 4.0 demonstrate the huge capacity that industry and traditional manufacturing have for change: vertical networking of smart production systems, horizontal integration via a new generation of global value chain networks, through-engineering across the entire value chain and the impact of exponential technologies.

- **Vertical networking of smart production systems**

The first main characteristic of Industry 4.0 is the vertical networking of smart production systems in the factories of the future.

This vertical networking uses cyber-physical production systems (CPPSs) to enable plants to react rapidly to changes in demand or stock levels and to faults. Smart factories organise themselves and enable production that is customer-specific and individualised. This requires data to be extensively integrated. Smart sensor technology is also needed to help with monitoring and autonomous organisation.

CPPSs enable not only autonomous organisation of production management but also maintenance management. Resources and products are networked, and materials and parts can be located anywhere and at any time. All processing stages in the production process are logged, with discrepancies registered automatically. Amendments to orders, fluctuations in quality or machinery breakdowns can be dealt with more rapidly. Such processes also enable wear and tear on materials to be monitored more effectively or pre-empted. All in all, waste is reduced.

Significant emphasis is attached to resource efficiency and in particular, the efficient use of materials, energy and human resources. The demands on workers engaged in operational tasks such as production, warehousing, logistics and maintenance are also changing, meaning that new skills in efficient working with CPPSs are required.

- **Horizontal integration via a new generation of global value chain networks**

The second main characteristic of Industry 4.0 is horizontal integration via a new generation of global value chain networks.

These new value-creation networks are real-time optimised networks that enable integrated transparency, offer a high level of flexibility to respond more rapidly to problems and faults, and facilitate better global optimisation.

Similar to networked production systems, these (local and global) networks provide networking via CPPSs, from inbound logistics through warehousing, production, marketing and sales to outbound logistics and downstream services. The history of any part or product is logged and can be accessed at any time, ensuring constant traceability (a concept known as 'product memory').

This creates transparency and flexibility across entire process chains—from purchasing through production to sales, for example, or from the supplier through the company to the customer. Customer-specific adaptations can be made not only in the production but also in the development, ordering, planning, composition and distribution of products, enabling factors such as quality, time, risk, price and environmental sustainability to be handled dynamically, in real time and at all stages of the value chain.

This kind of horizontal integration of both customers and business partners can generate completely new business models and new models for cooperation, representing a challenge for all those involved. Legal issues and questions of liability and protection of intellectual property are becoming increasingly important.

- **Through-engineering across the entire value chain**

The third main characteristic of Industry 4.0 is cross disciplinary through engineering across the entire value chain and across the full life cycle of both products and customers.

This engineering occurs seamlessly during the design, development and manufacture of new products and services. New products need new and/ or modified production systems. The development and manufacture of new products and production systems is integrated and coordinated with product life cycles, enabling new synergies to be created between product development and production systems.

Characteristic of this through-engineering is that data and information are also available at all stages of a product's life cycle, enabling new, more flexible processes to be defined from data via modelling to prototypes and the product stage.

- **Acceleration through exponential technologies**

The fourth main characteristic of Industry 4.0 is the impact of exponential technologies as an accelerant or catalyst that allows individualised solutions, flexibility and cost savings in industrial processes.

Industry 4.0 already requires automation solutions to be highly cognitive and highly autonomous. AI, advanced robotics and sensor technology have the potential to increase autonomy further still and to speed up individualisation and flexibilisation.

AI cannot only help to plan driverless vehicle routes in factories and warehouses more flexibly, save time and cost in SCM, increase reliability in production or analyse big data, but can also help to find new construction and design solutions or enhance the cooperation between humans and machines to the point of services.

Functional nanomaterials and nanosensors can also be used in production control functions to make quality management more efficient or allow the production of next generation robots that work 'hand in hand' and safely with humans.

Flying maintenance robots in production halls and using drones to make inventories of warehouse stock levels and deliver spare parts, at any time of day or night and in any terrain and weather, are further applications that will become simply routines in the autonomous and smart factories of the future.

A prime example here of an exponential technology that is accelerating Industry 4.0 and making it more flexible is 3D printing (additive manufacturing). 3D printing allows new production solutions (e.g. functionality, higher complexity without additional cost) or new supply chain solutions (e.g. inventory reduction, faster delivery times), or a combination of both that lead to disruptive new business models (e.g. disintermediation of supply chain members, customer integration).

More important will be the scanning for quality assurance or changes in SCM and warehousing through on-location printing of spare parts. Significant questions still need to be answered regarding intellectual property, product liability, customs duty and value-added tax.

While 3D printing already exists for all materials (metal, plastic, ceramic, living cells, etc.), not all materials fulfil industry requirements with regards to porosity and other characteristics. In the cases where the required quality has already been achieved, long lasting material qualification processes are under way, comparable with the processes for any other new material.

1.3   Industry 4.0: Challenges and Opportunities

In the current context characterised by the worlwide industries is facing substantial economic challenges due to an increasing pace of societal and technological development, such as a decreasing availability of natural resources, increasing energy prices, increasing age of employees and globalisation of markets. Moreover, customer increasingly demands for improved product-service innovation, product variety, quality standards, support services and immediacy of satisfaction.

These challenges need industrial enterprises that are capable of managing their whole value-chain in an agile and responsive manner. Companies need virtual and physical structures that allow for close cooperation and rapid adaption along the whole lifecycle from innovation to production and distribution.

The fourth industrial revolution or Industry 4.0 is called to pull applications and push technologies enabling a high degree of sustainability needed in the factories of the future (Kagermann 2015). As explained by (Kagermann et al. 2013), Industry 4.0 solves today challenges related with resources and energy efficiency, urban production and demographic change, enabling continuous resource productivity and efficiency.

One of the main pushed technologies are Internet-based and Internet of Services, favoured by new developments in computational power, leading to cloud computing and services. These technologies have the potential to give rise to a new generation of service-based industrial systems whose functionalities reside on-device and in-cloud. In order to succeed developing these technologies and applications, talented personnel, comprehensive IT infrastructure, economic strength and enlightened manufacturers will be needed. Industrial cloud-based cyber-physical systems. The IMC-AESOP Approach),[3] closing the loop for sustainable production systems.

Kagermann et al. (2013) describe Industry 4.0 as a collection of following seven concepts: smart factories, cyber-physical systems, self organisation, new systems in distribution and procurement, new systems in the development of products and services, adaptation to human needs and corporate social responsibility.

Hermann states that one characteristic of an Industry 4.0 factory is its ability to foresee future products and to respond to the variety and complexity intensification with low cost and low environmental impact.

1.4   *The Companies in Worldwide Framework of Industry 4.0*

The project Industrie 4.0 in a Global Context: Strategies for Cooperating[4] (2016) with International Partners was funded by the Federal Ministry for Economic Affairs and Energy (BMWi). It analyses the prospects for international cooperation in digital, connected industry.[5]

Based on the findings of an empirical survey of experts from six industrialised nations, it analyses both the opportunities and challenges for international cooperation in the field of Industrie 4.0 and the issues relating to the development of common norms and standards. The study is

---

[3] Cited also, available from Masters thesis-latest; Industry 4.0 & competitive advantage (Final) Henrik Paasikivis152449.docx.

[4] Available from https://www.plattform-i40.de/I40/Redaktion/EN/Downloads/Publikation/industrie-40-ina-global-context.pdf?__blob=publicationFile&v=1.

[5] The study's focus is based on the results of the project Industrie 4.0—International Benchmark, Future Options and Recommendations for Production Research (INBENZHAP), which was also funded by the BMWi. Among other things, this project recommended that German businesses should cooperate with international partners and that Germany should play a leading role in the field of standardisation.

based on over 150 interviews and conversations with experts from Germany, China, Japan, South Korea, the United Kingdom and the United States conducted between September 2015 and June 2016.

The results of the survey show that many countries share a very similar understanding of Industrie 4.0 (Industry 4.0 in german language), despite differences in their specific focus. The term Industrie 4.0 has also become established as a global brand. The experts from all of the countries in the study primarily associated Industrie 4.0 with networking and digitalisation. Other themes associated with the term included smart products, production optimisation, automation and new business models.

Businesses in particular are not simply introducing and adapting to Industrie 4.0 for the sake of it—they are doing so because of the economic opportunities that it provides. The experts from all of the countries saw production optimisation as one of the main economic benefits. This was by far the most frequently cited benefit in Germany, South Korea and the United Kingdom, reflecting the strong manufacturing focus of Industrie 4.0 in these countries. Automation is also regarded as extremely important. The experts from all the focus countries expected the resulting productivity gains to significantly increase their global competitiveness and strengthen manufacturing industry in their respective nations.

However, there were differences in how they rated the other economic opportunities of Industrie 4.0. In Germany in particular, there is a focus on combining information, communication and manufacturing technologies in smart, self-organising factories. In the United States and China, meanwhile, there is also a strong emphasis on smart products. While interviewees from the United States most frequently cited the significant potential for new business models, it is also recognised in Germany, Japan and increasingly China. The experts from the United States also hope that Industrie 4.0 will lead to better customer service, whereas in China they expect it to expand their product and service portfolio. Overall, the experts who took part in the survey considered one of the main strengths of the term Industrie 4.0 to be its holistic conceptual basis.

The experts from the United States were particularly conscious of the economic opportunities in the field of platform economies and emerging ecosystems. Financially strong, globally networked venture capital providers, innovative Silicon Valley start-ups and established software and Internet firms are all increasing their strategic focus on the market for Industrie 4.0 solutions. In China, the government initiatives Made in China 2025 and InternetPlus establish a contextual link between networking, integration and new, platform-based business models. The size of both the US and Chinese markets provides these countries with an advantage insofar as it enables local companies to rapidly grow their domestic market in order to generate the critical mass of customers and complementary products needed to take full advantage of future opportunities for global growth.

In this respect, the World Economic Forum establishes, in *The Global Information Technology Report 2013; Growth and Jobs in a Hyperconnected World*, a direct correlation between investment in digitalisation and GDP in an economy, in such a way that an increase of 10% in the digitalisation of a country generates an increase of 0.75% in GDP per capita and a decrease of 1.02% in the unemployment rate.

So, the European Commission Growth (2015) "Digital Transformation of European Industry and Enterprises", report from the Strategic Policy Forum on Digital Entrepreneurship[6] considers Digital Transformation to be key to Europe's ability to maintain its position of leadership in competitiveness (through the reduction of costs and the increased production) and the creation of stable, qualified employment. In a globalised world in which emerging countries are growing at rates that far outstrip the European Union, maintaining these lines of leadership is one of the biggest challenges for the Old Continent.

According to the study completed by the McKinsey Global Institute (2016), *Digital Europe, Pushing the Frontier, Capturing the Benefits*, it is estimated that a digitalisation of Europe (which currently stands at only 12% of potential) would contribute 2.5 billion euros to the economy by 2025, which would constitute 10% of current growth forecasts. To achieve these objectives, the European Commission makes the following recommendations:

1. Accelerate the use of *big data* and establish competitive digital platforms.
2. Update the digital training of professionals.
3. Promote the cities and regions as drivers of Digital Transformation.
4. Turn politicians, regulators and civil servants into ambassadors of Digital Transformation.

[6]Available from http://www.europarl.europa.eu/RegData/etudes/BRIE/2015/568337/EPRS_BRI(2015)568337_EN.pdf.

Along this line, the initiative of the commission itself to achieve a single digital market that might be considered very positive, but the reality is that the level of digitalisation of the EU is far from satisfactory. Only 16% of European SMEs use the Internet as a sales channel and, of these, fewer than half sell beyond the borders of their State. Moreover, Europeans do not have a very good level of digital competence (something which, we will see, is key in Digital Transformation): 45% of the population lack basic digital knowledge.

The countries with the highest levels of digitalisation (Denmark, Netherlands, Sweden and Finland) are leaders in this area also at world level, but the level of penetration of digital technology in companies varies greatly between EU Member States. Taking the EU as a whole, the data provided previously reveal that European companies are adapting at too slow a pace of change and are running the risk of being left behind.

If we take into account that over recent decades the economies that have shown the biggest commitment to new technologies are those that have most improved (Singapore, Finland, Norway, Sweden and the United States, leaders of NRI 2016, they are among the 10 economies with the highest income per capita), the fact that a level of digital development below that of the countries in our economic environment puts us in a vulnerable position.

2   DISRUPTIVE TECHNOLOGIES

2.1   *Technological Evolution and Training-Business Strategy*

No discussion on productivity and growth at present is complete without mentioning one of the key drivers: ICTs. Innovation in industry is more rapid, more complex and interlinked than ever. Companies that cannot handle the changes brought by ICTs will not be able to survive over the coming decades. The mobility, bandwidth, development of platforms and metadata are shaping the face of the company through rapid innovation. From new companies to more entrenched conglomerates, ICTs and their innovations and advances are shaking up the economy. The widespread dissemination of this technology through industry and sectors ensures that no aspect of the new economy can remain intact without evolving (ICT Workforce Study 2013). One aspect of the changing technology panorama is digitalisation: the widespread adoption of connected digital services on the part of consumers, companies and governments.

Various authors agree in pointing out that technologies associated with Industry 4.0 are, therefore, subject to integration with the following plans associated with the Digital Strategy:

- ADDITIVE MANUFACTURING: Distributed design and 3D printing.
- CLOUD COMPUTING: Applications, public models, private and hybrid. Virtualisation of infrastructures.
- INTERNET OF THINGS: Micro devices. Commercial applications. Wireless networks.
- COLLABORATIVE ROBOTICS: Cobots. Typology of robots. Artificial vision and environment perception.
- DATA ANALYSIS AND ARTIFICIAL INTELLIGENCE: Big Data. Automatic learning models. Distributed systems. Advanced Techniques for Data Analysis. Business Intelligence.
- BLOCKCHAIN: Bitcoin blocks explorer. P2P protocols and distributed trust.
- VIRTUAL AND AUGMENTED REALITY: Projection, levels and optical devices, etc.
- CYBERSECURITY: Encryption and steganography Types of attacks. Prevention, control and post-attack measures.
- SENSORS, ACTUATORS AND INTEGRATED SYSTEMS: Microcontrollers. Beacons. Communication sensors and protocols.
- PRODUCTION ENGINEERING AND DIGITAL VALUE CHAIN: Process Design and Management. Automated factories. Consumer-focussed factories. Encapsulated e-factories. Production and interoperability execution systems.
- HUMAN-MACHINE INTERACTION: Cognitive theories. Design of interfaces. Ethics and design and interaction methodologies. Assistant and augmentative technologies.
- FLEXIBLE PRODUCT DESIGN: Conceptualisation of products and user experience. Tools; Swift Kanban, Kanbanize, Scrum, Versión one, Pivotal Tracker and Trello, among others.
- SMART LOGISTICS: Localisation methods and applications. Automated route optimisation. Interoperable IoT systems.

Said training programmes must also integrate the relevant "key concepts";

DIGITAL TRANSFORMATION: New business models. Strategic impact of automation Risks map. Scorecards and Key Performance Indicators (KPIs). Financial impact. HR management. Digital Marketing. Leadership and Digital Reputation.

Along with the "key concept" TECHNOLOGICAL ENTERPRISE; Smart technology and opportunity analysis. Innovation. Improvement of processes. Financing enterprise.

And, as is obvious, the "key concept" of INDUSTRY 4.0, encompasses learning objectives such as the following:

- Obtain a general vision of Industry 4.0 (Digital Transformation of industrial companies and involvement in change of human resources).
- Find more relevant facilitating technologies in the connected industry, identifying the general foundations, the characteristics, uses, applications and real functioning example.
- Approach basic concepts and practical cases geared towards ascertaining:
  - Origin and current situation (4th Industrial Revolution).
  - State of the "Industry 4.0" question in the different industrial sectors
  - Facilitative and manufacturing technologies and optimisation of processes.
  - Digital Transformation of manufacturing (Factory 4.0 concept).
  - Redesign of processes and ways of working.
  - Continuous training and talent activation strategies.
  - The circular economy, efficiency and industrial sustainability.

2.2   *Challenges for Business Leaders*

Finally, and according to the mentioned authors before,

- Business leaders will need to determine when, how, and whether to take advantage of new technologies—and be prepared to move quickly when others use emerging technologies to mount challenges.
- Adopting disruptive technologies entails risks, and managing these risks will be critically important. Internally, organisational effectiveness and cohesion could suffer as some jobs are transformed—or eliminated—by technology. By working with employees

and redesigning jobs to focus on higher-value skills—and by investing in workforce development—companies can minimise these risks. External risks include reputational risk and consumer resistance, as well as safety and regulatory issues.

- Business leaders need to strike a careful balance as they adopt new technologies; they must be thoughtful about risk, but they should also manage these risks without stifling potential.

REFERENCES

European Commission Growth. (2015). 'Digital Transformation of European Industry and Enterprises' – Report from the Strategic Policy Forum on Digital Entrepreneurship. Brussels. Retrieved October, 2017, from http://ec.europa.eu/growth/content/digital-transformation-european-industry-and-enterprises-%E2%80%93-report-strategic-policy-forum-0_en.

ICT Workforce Study. (2013). *Australian Workforce and Productivity Agency.* Retrieved October, 2018, from https://docs.education.gov.au/documents/report-ict-workforce-study-july-2013.

Kagermann, H. (2015). Change Through Digitization-Value Creation in the Age of the Industry 4.0. In H. Albach, H. Meffert, A. Pinkwart, & R. Reichwald (Eds.), *Management of Permanent Change* (pp. 23–45). New York: Springer.

Kagermann, H., Wahlster, W., & Helbig, J. (2013). *Securing the Future of German Manufacturing Industry. Recomendations for Implementing the Strategic Initiative Industrie 4.0.* Frankfurt: Acatech-National Academy of Science and Engineering. Retrieved October, 2016, from http://www.acatech.de/fileadmin/user_upload/Baumstruktur_nach_Website/Acatch/root/de/Material_fuer_Sonderseiten/Industrie_4.0/Final_report__Industrie_4._accessible.pdf.

McKinsey Global Institute. (2016). *Digital Europe: Pushing the Frontier, Capturing the Benefits.* In collaboration with Digital Mckinsey. Retrieved October, 2018, from https://www.mckinsey.com/~/media/McKinsey/Business%20Functions/McKinsey%20Digital/Our%20Insights/Digital%20Europe%20Pushing%20the%20frontier%20capturing%20the%20benefits/Digital-Europe-Full-report-June-2016.ashx.

Nilsson, N. J. (2010). *The Quest for Artificial Intelligence: A History of Ideas and Achievements.* Cambridge, UK: Cambridge University Press.

Panetta, K. (2017). *Contributor To: Gartner Top 10 Strategic Technology Trends for 2018.* Retrieved March, 2018, from https://www.gartner.com/smarterwithgartner/gartner-top-10-strategic-technology-trends-for-2018/.

Werner, Struth B., & Shead, S. (2013). Industry 4.0: The Next Industrial Revolution. Retrieved October, 2018, from http://www.europarl.europa.eu/studies.

CHAPTER 2

The New Economy and New Business Models

This chapter tackles the definition of New Economy, its main elements and its transformation, a theoretical perspective, the economics of digital information; negligible marginal costs, network externalities and barriers and enablers of business model change.

Digital business models; origins, concept, guidelines to develop a consensus for the business models and Digital Business Models best practices identified are also outlined.

The chapter draws to a close with the key information regarding the main characteristics for E-Business Environment: generic e-Business Strategies, new Strategies for E-Organizations and new Digital Business Models for E-Organizations.

1 NEW ECONOMY DEFINITION AND MAIN ELEMENTS

The world economy is undergoing a fundamental structural change driven by the globalization of business on the one hand and by the revolution in information and communication technology on the other. The New Economy is the superior economic structure that is expected to arise as an outcome of these two forces.

In the late 1990s, many business leaders, investors, journalists and politicians became firmly convinced about the fact that the world economy is undergoing a fundamental structural change driven by both globalization and the revolution in ICT. The superior economic structure expected to

A. Landeta Echeberria, *A Digital Framework for Industry 4.0*, https://doi.org/10.1007/978-3-030-60049-5_2

arise as an outcome of these two forces was coined the 'New Economy' in the business press. The argument was simply that a business firm, an industry or an economy, which is able to successfully utilize these global trends, would eventually outperform its rivals. And, indeed, the casual evidence for the New Economy was strong. The stock market boomed, powered by ICT and 'dotcom' companies. Productivity and economic growth as well, took off in the United States. As a consequence, even average Americans warmed up to the idea that there really is a New Economy. According to an opinion poll conducted in March 2000, 57% of them believed that the United States has entered 'a new kind of an economy' that is 'significantly different from the industrial economy' (Business Week 2000).

The New Economy definition was coined by the business press to mean two broad trends in the world economy that have been under way for some time (Shepard 1997).

Three explanations can be given:

1. Firstly, a technological breakthrough seems to have occurred in the mid-1990s in semiconductor manufacturing as this industry shifted from a 3-year product cycle to a 2-year one (Jorgenson 2001).
2. The second explanation is the increase in network computing due to the rapid diffusion of a widespread information infrastructure—the Internet.
3. The third explanation for the interest in the New Economy is the fact that labour productivity appears to have picked up in the United States in the mid-1990s.

• **Economic growth**

According to (Jalava and Pohjola 2008), the New Economy represents an unquestionable economic growth. These authors point out that the ways in which ICT can enhance economic growth and then assess the impacts of the use and production of ICT on economic growth in a number of industria countries. By surveying recent research findings based on growth accounting analyses, they confirm that both these factors have been behind the improved economic performance of the United States in the 1990s. About two-thirds of the recent improvement in labour productivity can be attributed to ICT. The benefits from use are likely to have exceeded the benefits from production. However, the evidence for the

New Economy is much weaker outside the United States. In the other G7 countries, the contributions to output growth from the use of ICT have generally been less than half of the contributions estimated for the US.

On the other hand, in terms of income and wealth inequality, information and communication technology is one of the factors often claimed to be behind the observed increase in income and wealth inequality. The popular view is that the impacts are large. For example, (Wolff 2001: 3) wrote in its recently published survey of the new rich that 'the past decade was probably the most exuberant period of wealth creation in human history. It also produced an unprecedented number of wealthy people'.

On the other side, (Wolff 2001) takes a look at the facts in the leading New Economy—the United States. The Economist (Wolff 2001: 3) wrote in "A survey of the new rich" (special report: The new wealth of nations) applying family income and wealth data from the period 1947–1998, he finds that income inequality has indeed increased sharply since the late 1960s. Inequality in household wealth first declined until the mid-1970s and then increased dramatically.

Nowadays companies have to survive in an environment characterized by permanently and fast developing markets plus the adaption to diverse national and international determining factors (Doppler and Lauterburg 2005). Those market changes open on one hand new potentials for growth. On the other hand there is an increasing insecurity within the companies in regard to future planning caused by the high dynamic and complexity of the markets (Zahn et al. 2000). Interconnectivity and mobility are the crucial keywords.

The success of companies depends on the ability to control processes, to obtain process knowledge, and to make the knowledge inside people's minds—the tacit knowledge—more and more available for the growth of the company and increasing their value. Consequently, companies were starting years ago with profound restructuring of their processes (transformation), both inside their company as well as company overspreading. Main objectives are (a) building up business networks and (b) reach high performance mobility. A leaner organizational structure while maintaining the strategic flexibility is one of many challenges in this context. But not each company is really successful. The goal of each transformation is to reach a level of self-transforming companies (Berger 2014). With this idea, transformation or change management will be deeply rooted in the company and works in all strategic and operative processes. Following, the adaptability of the company to the permanently changing framework conditions can be reached. Future orientation and security is a consequence (Albach et al. 2014). The key factors are the people (in the digital world "users") and adaption of the technology.

On the other hand, there are many companies, which reach no added value with the transformation. A global survey by the MIT Center for Digital Business shows that only 15% of those questioned can say that they start proactive into the process of Digital Transformation (Westerman et al. 2011). Those protagonists are indeed more successful than their competitors. A main reason is that these companies have a clear goal, a vision. Against that it is difficult for companies, which are forced (by markets, by customers, etc.) to find a decent way transforming their company. Fact is that DBT is characterized by successful projects but also by failures.

But how work these transformations? Which processes act behind? The big goal seems to be clear: A transformed company in which all core processes are digitalized. That seems to be logically. For all that it is necessary to respect that the digital technologies are an enormous challenge for companies, because it leads to changes the way people live and work. The digital world is characterized by ubiquitous availability of information, social virtualization, absolute mobility, permanent availability, localization, and capable technologies (Consulting 2014). Digital media are nowadays immense advanced in the private sector (digital society), the individual's personal life; partly more intensive than at work. From this direction develops incomprehension and pressure for the non-digital company. But on the other hand people are prepared to use digital media.

Consequently, the changes go in following directions: relocation of the services from physical to digital; business interactions are more and more related to the social networks; digitalization and digital communication are part of the lifestyle and become consequently part of the business culture; working places are not only the desktop; intercontinental/global cooperation is a normal process; permanent changes are part of the daily life. This process of digitalization brings on one-hand risks by other (aggressive) market players. On the other hand there are lots of chances in three dimensions:

- More efficient business processes (new products and services).
- Increase in sales.
- Intensification of customer relationship.

Each company is situated more or less intensively in the progression of digitalization. To measure this, the process of strategy Digital Maturity Model TM (DBT) includes several dimensions in which the companies need to reach a level of competence.

Therefore, the dStrategy DBT TM defines the six dimensions Human Resources (grade of work with digital technology, management), Technology Resources (technologies for support of digitalization, grade of use), Data Strategy (capture, store, manage and use information), Content Strategy (create, manage, deliver, share and archive/renew content), Channel Strategy (Marketing/Communication, Transaction, Distribution), and Social Business Strategy (digital interaction and collaboration) which are scored in the levels zero, low, medium and high (Kubrick 2013).

Another view onto these competences is developed by (Rossman et al. 2014) defines eight dimensions in the digital maturity which are categorized in the levels Unaware, Conceptual, Defined, Integrated and Transformed:

- D1 – **Strategy**: the Consciousness for the Digital Transformation must be embedded in the company strategy.
- D2 – **Leadership**: the transformation needs leadership and should not be outsourced.
- D3 – **Products**: digitalization leads to new products and services with benefits for customers and new fields of business.
- D4 – **Operations**: the digitalization of the core processes has to be forced by a new operating model, which increases the agility inside the organization.
- D5 – **Culture**: a change of culture inside the company is necessary which leads to an open innovation culture.
- D6 – **People**: digitalization needs experts and digital qualification for the non-experts.
- D7 – **Governance**: Digital Strategy must become part of the objective agreement.
- D8 – **Technology**: replacement of older IT-structures is necessary.

In this sense, we cannot ignore the phenomenon of Globalization—as we pointed out in Chap. 4 of this study, and as one of the main characteristics of knowledge-based economies.

Globalization exerts its influence on the economic, political, cultural, social and environmental fields in every country. Its impact, however, differences from country to country, and from field to field.

Given their pursuit of super benefits based on scientific-technological achievements, transnational corporations are considered the midwives for the birth of the globalization of the world economy (Phan Doan Nam 1998).

According to *The knowledge based economy: facts and figures* (OECD 1999), the knowledge-based economy have the following fundamental features:

1. The knowledge-based economy as the most decisive factor in production.
2. Rapid restructuring.
3. Information technology and telecommunications widely applied in all aspects of socioeconomic life.
4. A learning society in which the education system is changing into a lifelong education experience.

Under the impact of the global information network, the traditional market has been undergoing profound changes, and is gradually adjusting itself to new developments of the knowledgebased economy.

The searching opportunities in the knowledge-based economy also brings about a fierce competitive environment.

- **Elements of the new economy**

It is because of that, within several implications for capital markets and labor, the main elements of New Economy are the following ones:

- New technology.
- New products.
- Productivity and Growth.
- Capital markets.
- Impact for labor.
- Regulation.
- Taxation and Political Economy.
- The International Division of Labor.

In this respect, the main characteristics of these elements, citing and summarising several authors are described as follows (Table 2.1).

2   DIGITAL BUSINESS MODEL TRANSFORMATION

Some examples of industries that are in midst of Digital Transformations included: banking and insurance, telecom, media and publishing in general, music and movies (Lucas et al. 2013). Whilst these technological advancements create tremendous opportunities for companies, especially new ventures, they simultaneously threaten and disrupt incumbents (Al-Debei et al. 2008a).

2.1   *Theoretical Perspective*

Business model

Digital business model broadly refers to the activities of a number of actors linked through ICTs to conceive economic value. (Zott and Amit 2010) building upon their earlier work (Amit and Zott 2001) define business models as depicting the 'content, structure, and governance of activity systems designed so as to create value through the exploitation of business opportunities" (Zott and Amit 2010). This conceptualization basically involves the what, how and who questions related to the activities. Activity system content refers to the selection of activities that are performed. Activity system structure concerns the way in which the activities are linked and their importance for the business models. Activity system governance refers to who performs the activities. This is by far the most well-established and comprehensive conceptualization of the business model notion in the literature for several reasons. First, it is the most theoretically and empirically grounded conceptualization of business model. (Amit and Zott 2001) lay theoretical foundations of the business model notion through investigating sources of value creation in 59 e-businesses. Second, its main focus on generation of economic value from the use of ICT unifies several contemporary theoretical strands (Schumpeterian innovation, value chain analysis, resource-based view of firm, transaction cost economics and strategic networks). As such it has the ability to account for the relevance and uniqueness of the digital realm, which other single theoretical bodies cannot. The conventional theories of value creation are intended to be firm centric and have been developed before the ICT revolution, to suit traditional organizations engaged in

Table 2.1 The main elements of new economy

	1. New technology. Technological innovation means a new production function:
	  – Capital markets.
	  – Labor.
	  – Regulation, and
	  – Taxation.
	2. Looking at the new economy from the technological angle, the essential change is a new technology. Internet represents a network system that connects millions of computers on a computed network (Engel 1999).

New products	3. New economy from the point of view of products, larger set of goods:
	  – New IT product.
	  – New technological device (input to production and consumption activities).
	  – Process innovation.
	4. Characteristics product "information":
	Information can be shared and yet it is not lost for the first "owner". Information displays "infinite expansibility" (Quah 1999).
	5. New good information relates to demand for the new product (Varian 1998; Shapiro and Varian 1998).
	6. Another related issue of the new product is information overload.
	7. New IT product means a new market.
	8. Pricing of network use is a major issue (McKnight and Bailey 1995).

Productivity and growth

9. A strong impact of the new technology and of information as a new product on the performance of the economy as a whole and on society can be expected.

10. A new product is produced: a logistical S-shaped curve. S-curve. The new IT product, which enlarges the product set of the economy, brings additional value added. An increase in factor income and in output. Producing and collecting, accumulating, processing, distributing and evaluating information represent new activities.

11. The new technology revolutionizes the organization of firms.

12. In the virtual economy, transportation costs are reduced because some of the products can now be transmitted via the Internet instead of being physically shipped.

13. The productivity is increased.

14. The production potential means that the economy moves to a higher growth path. A higher level and the transition path with a higher GDP level as well.

15. Changes in society, new "culture".

16. The macroeconomic impact the new economy.

17. The productivity paradox. IT-revolution represents a technological breakthrough like the railroads in the nineteenth century and the automobile in the twentieth century. Different approaches can be taken to determine the productivity effect.

  – First approach it to collect data on where the new technology is adopted.

  – Second approach is to estimate the firm's production function and to determine the output elasticity of IT-capital.

  – Third approach is to is to use a macroeconomic production function and to account for the determinants of economic growth with special reference to the new economy.

18. The new economy means a strong sectoral change towards the information society continuing the secular trend away from the industrial economy to the service economy.

19. The business cycle, a new cycle, a new Kondratieff cycle[a]. This does not imply that the business cycle is dead. The components of aggregate demand may still move in a cyclical way, and slumps cannot be excluded even if the capacity constraint becomes more flexible.

20. Supply side.

(continued)

Table 2.1 (continued)

Capital markets	21. The capital markets have to provide capital to the new firms, which have to build up a new capital stock. The high stock market prices do not reflect profits, and the price-earning ratio is not founded on a high actual rate of return. US, estimates are that the firms of the new economy make up 10% of GDP whereas market capitalization is at 30% (Dornbusch 2000: 24). 22. To what extent, the high market capitalization of the new firms represents a bubble. The emergence of a new sector means a Schumpeterian process of restructuring and of creative destruction. Other sectors will decline, at least in relative terms, and capital will flow to the new sectors. It will take time until the new firms add to the total value of the stock market; as a first effect the market value of existing firms that are negatively affected by the new firms is likely to decline (Greenwood and Jovanovic 1999).
Impact for labor	23. Demand for labor is a derived demand. In the information industry, it is no longer the dexterity of the craftsman at the assembly line, nor is it any longer the friendly smile at the service counter, that are essential, it is ideas, creativity, associative power, it is brain. We have a different type of production function with human capital as the decisive factor o production. 24. There are implications for the realm of work in the traditional sectors of the economy. The organization of work changes, there is an increased decentralized responsibility with more autonomy at the decentralized level and requiring more flexibility. 25. Human capital is decisive. The new economy implies a further shift in relative demand in favor of qualified labor and to the disadvantage of less qualified labor. In order to prevent a digital divide in the work force, building up human capital is an important strategy for society as well. 26. The implications for the institutional arragements are sizable. If countries want to be competitive in the new economy, they have to change their institutional set-up. 27. The trade unions means that their environment abruptly changes. 28. To what extent the new technology will affect employment and unemployment. We expect labor productivity to increase; this implies a higher demand for qualified labor. The IT-sector needs qualified people for producing and servicing hardware and software and producing information. The higher income will increase the demand for services and non-tradables in a general way.

Regulation

29. The new economy needs an appropiate instituiconal set-up. (Engel 1999). Patents give a strong property right for a limited time and grant the winner of the patent a quasi-monopolistic position. It excludes others from the markets. The stronger the property right, the stronger the incentive to invent, but the greate the losses from the monopolistic position (Shapiro and Varian 1998).

30. Antitrust policy.
   With respect to the new product "information" suppliers of information will attempt to appropriate it and to make it exclusive but it is unlikely that in this area of information products monopolistic positions will develop. After all, market entry at low costs is possible for information providers.

31. The network itself must be regulated. Carriers have been considered to be natural monopolies. The new literature, however, has correctly pointed out that property rights can be defined for quite a few common carriers. The Internet now exists as the result of private activity. There does not seem to be a need for too much regulation. Some standardization is necessary, but this was obtained by voluntary protocols. Other legal issues relate to privacy, decency and free speech, fraud and security, encryption and junk mail.

32. Traditional Telecommunication sector.

33. International aspects of regulation arise.

(continued)

Table 2.1 (continued)

Taxation and Political Economy	34. The government taxes the private sector because it needs money for the purposes of allocation (the provision of public goods) and of distribution.
	35. The IT sector is taxed like the other sectors of the economy: – Highly mobile internationally. – Highly qualified human capital. The local activities cannot avoid the national taxes.
	36. Indirect taxation. The difficulty of the EU-countries to collect the value added tax from the new economy. The new EU-directive attempts to solve that problem in analogy to the mail-order business.
	37. Specific taxation of the IT-sector is another issue (within the allocation branch of government, benefit taxation or charges for using the infrastructure represent specific reasons for raising government revenue).
	38. Auctioning of licenses.
	39. The IT technology may affect political power and change the politica economy.
The International Division of Labor	40. The new economy represents a new technology that will be associated with a higher growth rate. For developing countries, new opportunities open up.
	41. It is especially important that they have qualified people and proper educational systems.

Source: Author's own from several authors in a synthetic way

[a]Long-duration economic cycle of major capital goods expansion that plays out over a period of about 60 years and underlies the usual boom-bust cycles characteristic of a capitalist economy. Named after its proponent, the Russian economist Nikolai Dmitrijewitsch Kondratieff (1892–1938). Also called long wave cycle. Source: http://www.businessdictionary.com/definition/Kondratieff-cycle.html

production of material products. Third, the focus on the activities is particularly important and it is what distinguishes it from other notions of business models in the literature and other concepts as well.

2.2   Economics of Digital Information

Transaction cost reduction

Transaction costs refers to the costs associated with completion of a transaction (Williamson 1983). These costs include search and information costs (costs involved in searching and finding relevant information regarding different products/services, communication, travel costs, prices, delivery schedule), production and inventory costs, bargaining costs (costs involved in the process of reaching agreement with other parties that partake in the transactions, drafting contracts) negotiating, contract drafting costs), policing and enforcement costs (costs related to contract safeguarding and supervision), costs associated to transportation with buying and selling and all the costs related to information processing that are required to coordinate the work performed by people and machines (Williamson 1983; Amit and Zott 2001).

ICT has proved to significantly reduce transaction costs (Dyer 1997). In the physical world, processes are organized into long and complex value chains that involve rather huge transaction costs, involving many middlemen between buyers and sellers. Digital businesses are characterized by a disintermediation process, since ICT enables faster and easier direct communication and connection between buyers and sellers.

2.3   Negligible Marginal Costs

Digital information products have a characteristic cost structure that is distinct from the traditional manufactured products. Marginal costs refer to the incurring costs to produce one more unit of a product or service (Shapiro and Varian 1998). The key costs arise mostly from the production, whereas reproduction of same products does not generate additional costs. Thus, production, reproduction and distribution of digital information products have very low marginal costs that in terms of the resources involved are equal to zero for digital network distribution.

2.4   Network Externalities

Another fundamental difference between the traditional material logic and digital products is that conventional economics is driven by economics of scale whereas digital economy is driven by the economics of networks. It specifically means that a particular product or service becomes more valuable when more people use it (Shapiro and Varian 1998). Network effects are the main driver of favouring or choosing one product over the other.

2.5   Barriers and Enablers of Business Model Change

Whilst business model change is not a recent phenomenon, the magnitude of innovation as a result of the digital technologies is incomparable.

There are three main processes that may enable successful business model innovation: experimentation, effectuation and leading change. Experimentation refers to testing the business models with real customers in real transactions. Another method to experimentation is discovery-driven planning (McGrath 2010), that refers to the ways of modelling unknown assumptions that can be directly tested and evaluated. On the other hand, effectuation represents a model of entrepreneurial decision-making in the absence of pre-existing markets. With this approach managers do not analyze the market as much as they enact it. A third success factor is the successful leadership of organizational change. This means that organizations need to know and have in place suitable agents that lead the change in organizations.

3   DIGITAL BUSINESS MODELS

Within the article "Digital business models: review and synthesis" define digital business concet as well as its origins. As we can see in the bibliographical references used by these authors in the following two sections. There is no accepted definition of the term "business model".

Others, in fact, some have argued that the concept of a business model is relatively new (Morris et al. 2005).

In addition, the concept of business models can be seen as having progressed in five stages as shown in figure (Gordijn et al. 2005).

3.1   Origins of Business Models

In general, there is no accepted definition of the term "business model". Although the concept had gained prominence only in the last decade or two. Many have observed that the term "business model" became widely adopted by practitioners during the dotcom revolution of the 1990s. While business model has been part of the business jargon for a long time, it has been argued that the focus initially involved a scientific analysis of firms has been on industry, and resources, as shown by the works of (Porter 1980) and Wernerfeld. Others, in fact, some have argued that the concept of a business model is relatively new, dating back to only the early 1980s. Furthermore, there is little theoretical underpinning in the literature particularly in economic theory.

A business model is a representation of the strategic choices that characterize a business venture. These choices are made either intentionally or by default, so the contribution of a business model is to make them explicit (Morris et al. 2005). The business model can be a communication or a planning tool.

- **New Architectures**

Responding to the velocity and turbulence of the environment, and taking advantages of the affordances of digital technology, firms and groups of *digital platforms* for the combination of technologies and the delivery of services.

Digital business ecosystems feature not only idiosyncratic technological architectures but also important new interorganizational business architectures. Responding to the velocity and turbulence of the environment, and taking advantages of the affordances of digital technology, firms and groups of firms have been prolific in establishing digital platforms for the combination of technologies and the delivery of services. Platforms are standards or architectures that allow modular substitution of complementary assets. Taking advantage of the digital affordance of modularity, platforms enable firms to focus their attention (and innovation) on one part of a system at a time, and to assemble those parts—whether they are products or activities—into a variety of configurations.

As business models have become more digital, firm capabilities themselves have become more modular, more easily connectable, and more conveniently shareable. In prior decades it might have taken a formal alliance and a joint venture to make one firm's technology compatible with another's, but today, riding on rails of application programming interfaces (APIs) and broadband fiber optics, we can 'mash up' digital services like Google's maps and Facebook's social newsfeed in no time and on a shoestring budget. Digital business ecosystems enable the possibility of combining capabilities across boundaries into innovative new offerings and solutions to create and capture value.

3.2   The Business Model Concept

Porter (2001) argues that a flood of new entrants has come into many industries since the Internet has reduced barriers to entry.

It is structured as follows. In the next section, we highlight the different viewpoints IS field researching into business models. We then present the four main concepts and values and their interaction, which position the BM within the organization.

As follows, the guidelines to developd a consensus for the business model definition and meaning.

As we have seen, despite the increasing emphasis on the importance of the business model to an organization's success, there has been a lack of consensus regarding its definition and its meaning. Researchers in this area have depicted business models from different perspectives. Through an analysis of definitions of the business model in the IS literature presented in the previous section, we propose the following reasons and guidelines for establishing a BM as a second level of clarity (Al-Debei et al. 2008b).

- A way in which organizations create value (Amit and Zott 2001) with two different approaches for the value proposition:
- The ways in which an organization, along with its suppliers and partners (business actors) creates value for its customers (Magretta 1998, 2002; Petrovic et al. 2001; Stähler 2002; Osterwalder 2005; Haaker et al. 2006).

- The ways in which an organization, along with its stakeholders (business actors), create value for each party involved (Bouwman 2002; Stähler 2002; Haaker et al. 2006).
- A way in which an organization generates revenue (Timmers 1998; Magretta 1998, 2002).
- An abstraction of the existing business and a future planned business (Stähler 2002). This suggests that the organization's business models should encompass future business outlooks.
- An architecture for the organization, including its assets, products, services, and information flow (Timmers 1998).
- As business logic relating to the ways in which businesses are being conducted (Petrovic et al. 2001; Osterwalder 2005).
- A way in which an organization enables transactions through the coordination and collaboration among parties and multiple companies (Amit and Zott 2001; Bouwman 2002; Haaker et al. 2006).
- An organization's strategy or set of strategies (Leem et al. 2004). An interface or a theoretical layer between the business strategy and the business processes (Campanovo and Pigneur 2003; Tikkanen et al. 2005; Rajala and Westerlund 2005; Morris et al. 2005).
- A conceptual tool, a business abstraction, and a blueprint (Stähler 2002; Haaker et al. 2004; Osterwalder 2005). A way of understanding a single organization or a network of organizations (Bouwman 2002; Haaker et al. 2006).

3.3   Best Practices: Digital Business Models

Some scholars, educators and consultants have agreed with Allan Greespan. So that, the common emerging e-business business models[1] are:

1. Business-to-Business (B2B).
2. Business-to-Consumer (B2C).
3. Customer-to-Business (C2B).

---

[1] Definitions available from http://reports.weforum.org/digital-transformation/wp-content/blogs.dir/94/mp/files/pages/files/digital-enterprisenarrative-final-january-2016.pdf.

4. Business-to-Government (B2G).
5. Government-to-Business (G2B).
6. Government-to-Government (G2G).
7. Business-to-Employee (B2E) and Employee-to-Business (E2B).

Dickson and DeSanctis (2001) summarized the Digital Business Models as follows:

1. Focused Distributors provide products and services related to a specific industry or market niche. There are five types: (a) retailers. (b) Market places. (c) Aggregators. (d) Exchanges, and (e) informediaries.
2. Portals, they serve as gateways and provide tools needed to connect to World Wide Web (e.g., AOL).
3. Product design, produce and sitribute products ands services that meet customer needs (e.g. manufacturers, serive providers, educators, advirsors).
4. Infrastructure portals are firms that provide consumers or businesses with access to a wide range of network, computation and application hosting.

4   CHARACTERISTICS FOR E-BUSINESS ENVIRONMENT

We can outline—according to—the characteristics of the E-Business Environment and Generic e-Business Strategies in the applicability of Porter's generic strategies in the digital age: Assumptions, conjectures and suggestions of Kim et al.

While Porter's typology has received a good deal of empirical support in traditional business contexts (Miller and Friesen 1986; Miller 1988), we do not know whether Porter's generic strategies or any other strategy typology can be applied to e-business firms. An extensive body of literature has already described the essential characteristics of the e-business environment and how it differs from and is similar to traditional business environments (e.g. Bakos 1997; Cross and Smith 1996; Porter 2001). Here, we highlight aspects of the e-business competitive landscape that are most relevant to the concept of competitive strategy.

How is e-business different? The Internet allows firms to overcome physical boundaries and distance and it also allows them to serve larger audiences more efficiently. At the same time, and perhaps more importantly, Web technologies allow companies to target specific consumer groups, which may be difficult to do in traditional markets due to the high cost of obtaining information about a particular customer segment. Furthermore, traditional marketing methods usually emphasize only one-way communication from marketers to consumers, while the Internet is an interactive medium (Yelkur and DaCosta 2001).

Our brief overview of the e-business landscape and these assumptions and necessary conditions suggest two plausible scenarios of competitive strategy: First, due to the power of search engines and the ease of making price comparisons, Internet retailers will be forced to charge essentially the same price, giving an advantage to successful cost leaders.

Alternatively, firms will strive to compete on factors other than price, giving an advantage to firms that employ successful differentiation strategies (Clay et al. 2002). In the following sections, we explore these strategic options and consider possible variations.

Cost Leadership Strategy

Cost leadership can be an obvious strategic choice for many e-business firms. Although lower costs do not necessarily mean lower prices, lower prices have been a key selling point for e-business firms like Expedia.com, CDnow, and many others, at least in the early stages of their development. The cost leadership strategy may be particularly appealing to online buyers who are price sensitive. In one study conducted in Korea, 71%of 500 first-time online shoppers indicated that price was their most important consideration. The Internet also allows firms to adjust their prices quickly so they can enjoy greater pricing flexibility and more efficient price competition (Bakos 1997).

The Internet also helps consumers overcome bounded rationality in terms of price scanning.

The longstanding satisfying argument may be less applicable in the Internet environment since the speed and expansiveness of information search on the Web enable consumers to quickly gather a wealth of data for price comparisons. Price comparison sites can further reduce search costs, so sophisticated Internet users can benefit from nearly perfect information acquired at little or no cost (Bakos 1997). Internet technologies also provide buyers with easier access to information about products and suppliers, thus bolstering buyer bargaining power (Porter 2001).

Differentiation Strategy

As noted above, differentiation can be based on many elements or factors, including design, brand image, reputation, technology, product features, networks and customer service.

Any successful differentiation strategy must be based on elements that are difficult for competitors to imitate. In spite of conditions that encourage e-business firms to compete on price, we believe that many if not all of these differentiating elements can also be used by e-businesses to distinguish themselves from competitors.

The Internet's lower switching costs should also encourage e-businesses to pursue a strategy of differentiation. In traditional businesses, consumers often tolerate mediocre products and services due to high switching costs. In the e-business environment, however, consumers can get access to information that was previously impossible to obtain or to compare, and can, with just a few mouse clicks, easily switch to firms that offer additional value through differentiated features (Kim 2000; Porter 2001). As a result, e-business retailers will gain advantage if they can offer differentiated products and services, and they must also seek additional ways to distinguish themselves (Miller 1991). In addition to traditional differentiating factors such as Brand image, product features, and customer service, many e-businesses are also differentiating their distribution channels by emphasizing speed of delivery, convenience and the security of transactions. (Amit and Zott 2001) concluded that trust and security can be keys to "locking-in" customer purchases and loyalty.

Focus Strategy

Firms pursuing a focus strategy target specific groups of buyers, product lines or geographic areas. Within their more limited market scope, they emphasize either low costs or differentiated products and services. Many Internet companies are new entrants, and they will logically choose to compete against large, established firms by focusing on a particular market niche. In addition, the lower levels of investment required by many online businesses means that they enjoy lower break-even points than competitors with higher levels of fixed costs. Thus, targeting even small market segments might be viable, and consumers may be easily connected with companies that focus on niche markets due to the Internet's search advantages.

4.1   Generic Strategies and E-Business Performance

Cost leadership is widely practised today among e-business firms that sell standardized products and services such as books (Barnesandnoble.com) and travel (Expedia.com).

Indeed, among first-time online shoppers, price may well be the most important factor influencing their buying decisions. This may be partially attributable to the ease of scanning and comparing prices on the Internet (Bakos 1997). However, easy price comparisons and very low customer switching costs suggest that firms pursuing a strategy of cost leadership could easily become locked in a vicious cycle of price-cutting.

Because the Internet is an open system, companies have more difficulty maintaining proprietary offerings, thus intensifying the rivalry among competitors. Internet technologies tend to reduce variable costs, tilting cost structures toward fixed cost and creating significantly greater pressure for companies to engage in destructive price competition (Porter 2001). In addition, firms pursuing cost leadership will turn to outside vendors that offer the same products and services to other firms, so that purchased inputs become more homogeneous, further eroding company distinctiveness and increasing price competition (Porter 2001). Since the Internet also mitigates the need for an established sales force or access to existing marketing and distribution channels, barriers to entry are further reduced. Given all of these drawbacks, (Merrilees 2001) concludes that, while low prices are important to customers, a generic strategy of cost leadership has many drawbacks for e-business firms.

Traditionally, cost leadership and differentiation or their equivalents were regarded as equally effective strategies (Porter 1980). We suggest otherwise. For obvious reasons, Price competition will almost certainly intensify in the Internet business environment, and firms with commodity-like products and services will face great pressure to keep their prices as low as possible. Therefore, the preferred strategy choice for firms wanting to survive on the Internet would be differentiation. Hence, we offer the following proposition:

Proposition 1 In e-business, the generic strategy of differentiation will be associated with higher performance than the generic strategy of cost leadership.

As discussed earlier, Internet technologies potentially give all online retailers the ability to target both broad and narrow customer segments. Firms that pursue narrowly focused strategies are unlikely to be as successful as firms pursuing either cost leadership or differentiation strategies because those firms can take advantage of the infinite scalability of Internet technologies to reach simultaneously both broad and narrow customer segments. So, unlike (Porter 1980), who argued that firms could viably serve very narrow market segments, we propose that firms pursuing strategies of focus cost leadership or focus differentiation will be less viable than firms that take advantage of the scalability of Internet technologies:

Proposition 2 In e-business, the generic strategy of focus will be less viable than the generic strategies of cost leadership or differentiation.

"Stuck in the Middle" Versus "Integrated" Strategies and E-Business Performance (Porter 1980) argued that cost leadership and differentiation are such fundamentally contradictory strategies, requiring such different sets of resources, that any firm attempting to combine them would wind up "stuck in the middle" and fail to enjoy superior performance.

From a traditional business perspective, cost leadership and differentiation do seem incompatible. Cost leadership requires standardized products with few unique or distinctive features or services so that costs are kept to a minimum. On the other hand, differentiation usually depends on offering customers unique benefits and features, which almost always increase production and marketing costs (Hitt et al. 2001).

Furthermore, turbulent global environments require firms to adopt flexible combinations of strategies (Chan and Wong 1999). Any incompatibility between cost leadership and differentiation may hold true in more stable environments, but rapidly changing competitive environments call for more flexibility and the ability to combine elements of more than one generic strategy. Mass customization and the development of network organizations both demand and make possible the flexible combination of multiple strategies (Anderson 1997; Pine 1993).

Evans and Wurster (1999) concluded that the Internet disassembles traditional value chains, introducing new competitive imperatives and requiring new strategies. One doesn't have to agree completely with these sweeping observations to accept that the Internet has reduced trade-offs between information richness and information reach, or that the Internet's universality and its ability to reduce information asymmetries and transactions costs have created opportunities to "rewrite the rules" of business strategy. Merrilees (2001) observed that several online companies have successfully employed a combination of cost leadership and differentiation, and Amazon.com is offered as a case in point. Amazon.com's skills at branding, innovation, and channel management have successfully differentiated it from its competitors, but the company routinely offers low list prices on much of its merchandise. As a result, it is difficult to classify Amazon.com into either strategy type. Amazon.com does emphasize low prices and offers many discounts, but it has also been very innovative. Amazon.com's Web site was designed around a straightforward five-step process that makes the consumer shopping experience convenient and helpful. Prompt delivery is also a hallmark of the Amazon.com shopping experience.

While we do not want to minimize the very real challenges of pursuing a successful combination of generic strategies (Uhlenbruck et al. 2001; Porter 1980), we believe that an integrated strategy combining elements of cost leadership and differentiation is not only possible but is the most successful strategy for e-business firms to pursue. As discussed in the previous section, the strategy of cost leadership suffers from many inherent disadvantages. It is thus likely to offer lower performance than an integrated strategy that combines the best features of cost leadership and differentiation. We also expect that an integrated strategy will have higher performance than a pure differentiation strategy, since a strategy of pure differentiation does not take advantage of the Internet's potential for lowering costs. Thus, we offer the following proposition:

Proposition 3 Integrated strategies combining elements of cost leadership and differentiation will result in higher performance than cost leadership or differentiation does individually.

Pure Plays, Clicks-and-Bricks and Firm Performance

Two broad types of Internet businesses exist: pure online firm (pure plays) and firms with both online and offline businesses (clicks-and-bricks). During the earlier stages of e-business, many observers believed pure plays would be in a stronger competitive position.

It was thought that pure plays would be more flexible and better able to leverage their first mover advantages, and that they would not be hindered by conflicts between online and traditional marketing channels.

They would also enjoy greater flexibility in pricing. Netscape provides a good example of a pure online firm that was able to seize a dominant share of the browser market by ignoring conventional rules (Yoffie and Cusumano 1999). Dell is another company that gained significant advantages by pursuing an online strategy. In fact, traditional offline firms, which joined the Internet as second movers, did struggle at first.

By the end of 1998, however, many of these firms were becoming market leaders. A recent market survey found that clicks-and-bricks firms such as Barnes & Noble, Toys 'R' Us, and KBKids are among the largest Internet shopping sites (Bulik 2000).

Advantages of Clicks-and-Bricks Firms

Since clicks-and-bricks firms are already familiar to customers and have credible brands, other things being equal, customers should prefer clicks-and-bricks Internet sites.

Brynjolfsson and Smith (2000) concluded that the brand recognition, reputation, and credibility of clicks-and-bricks firms are important advantages that pure plays often lack. Furthermore, clicks-and-bricks firms can offer product returns and other customer services through their physical storefronts (Griffith 1999). Zettlemeyer (1996) showed that clicks-and-bricks firms could enjoy higher performance by properly combining their online and offline businesses, whereas the ability of pure plays to provide information would be limited to their online channel. In fact, recently many pure plays are realizing the advantages of adding offline elements such as warehousing (Glover et al. 2001).

Modahl (2000) concluded that e-business would be dominated by clicks-and-bricks, particularly by established firms that expand online by leveraging their offline assets such as distribution channels, brand reputation, and credibility. Support for this perspective comes from an empirical study by (Uhlenbruck et al. 2001), which found that "old economy firms" could achieve positive market returns by acquiring Internet firms.

Office Depot has employed the Web to improve its catalog services. Without printing more catalogs, the company's customers can access updated and accurate information through the Web and complete transactions online. Walgreen's, which has established an online site for ordering prescriptions, has found that its extensive network of stores remains a potent advantage, even as much prescription ordering shifts to the Internet. Fully 90% of the company's customers who place orders over the Web prefer to pick up their prescriptions at a nearby Walgreen's store rather than have them shipped to their homes, most likely to save shipping costs. The Gap's online customers will find an almost seamless integration between the company's Web site and the product offerings at its physical stores (Head et al. 2000).

Tight integration between a company's Web site and its physical store locations not only increases customer value, but it can also reduce costs. It is more efficient to take and process orders via the Web, but it is also more efficient to make bulk deliveries to a local stocking location than to ship individual customer orders from a central warehouse (Porter 2001). A recent article in The Wall Street Journal noted that many clicks-and-bricks firms are encouraging customers to pick up merchandise ordered online at their physical store locations. Not only does customer pick up save what are often substantial shipping charges (especially on large or heavy items), but companies also find that customer pick up leads to more impulse purchases. The article cited an executive at REI who estimated that "online shoppers who pick up their items in stores spend an additional $90 before they walk out the door" (Xiong 2003: D4).

Furthermore, many customers have used the Internet as a source of product and service information, but still prefer to make their purchases through traditional channels (Yang and Jun 2002). If this customer segment remains large, then clicks-and-bricks firms will enjoy further advantages over pure plays.

Pure plays face a number of other drawbacks. First, their customers cannot physically examine, touch, and test products, and they often get little or no help in using or repairing them. In addition, knowledge transfer is restricted to codified knowledge, sacrificing the spontaneity and judgment that can result from interactions with skilled sales personnel. It's always possible that advances in Internet technology will allow pure plays to offer highly personalized customer service—Amazon.com with its personalized customer recommendations offers an example of what is currently possible—but the lack of human contact with customers eliminates a powerful tool for responding to questions, providing advice, and motivating purchases. Finally, the lack of a physical storefront, fixtures, and amenities limits the ability of pure play firms to reinforce a brand image (Porter 2001).

Potential Problems Faced by Clicks-and-Bricks

Clicks-and-bricks firms also face a number of drawbacks. First, unless on- and offline operations are tightly integrated, a firm will see few synergies from having both an online and a physical presence. For example, Barnes & Noble's decision to spin-off Barnesandnoble. com as a separate organization is now viewed as a mistake. It prevented the online store from capitalizing on the many advantages provided by Barnes & Noble's network of physical stores (Porter 2001). Similarly, visitors to theWeb site of Angus and Robertson, an upscale Australian book retailer, are likely to be confused by the low prices emphasized by the company's online store, since this theme is inconsistent with the upmarket positioning of the company's physical stores (Merrilees 2001).

Old economy companies—those that were not created to employ an Internet business model but instead have added Web activities to their traditional operations—face considerable hurdles in establishing online operations. Not surprisingly, Scott and Walter found that the most serious problem facing these old economy companies is strategy related, specifically, the need to effectively align their e-business and traditional strategies.

All in all, at this stage of evolution, it appears that clicks-and-bricks firms can enjoy a number of advantages over pure plays, but to realize these advantages, they must effectively integrate their online and physical operations. Pure plays face all of the difficulties of establishing online operations (e.g. intense rivalry, pressure to lower prices, and the difficulty of establishing brand name recognition), without any of the opportunities to leverage their online operations with offline assets that clicks-and-bricks firms enjoy. Based on these arguments, we offer a final proposition:

Proposition 4 In e-business, the relationship between strategy and performance will be mediated by type of firm, with clicks-and-bricks firms that tightly integrate their on- and offline operations enjoying performance advantages over pure play firms.

4.2   New Digital Business Models for E-Organizations

This researcher postulates the following x-business hybrid model, which includes current e-business models and best business practices.

There is no cookie cutter model to fit every possible business scenario. However, managers and entrepreneurs should invest some time and resources in developing an x-business, model to meet their business needs and customers' expectations.

The future will be more challenging for managers without new skill sets trying to develop e-business models and strategies on their own. The rate of change in the new economy will make some the current sill sets obsolet or disposable (throw away). Most managers will be forced to reinvent them to remain competitive in the job market. However, managers can work together with academia and professionals in other industries to succed in a turbulent global economy and virtuous work place (Cuffe 2005).

4.3 New Strategies for E-Organizations

The following methodology can assist managers in navigating the change process (Ball et al. 2004) (Table 2.2).

This researcher believes that a hybrid strategy (i.e. combination of old and new economy tools) will be required to meet the challenges in the emerging global economy.

Managers should use Fr Michael E. Porter's Competitive Analysis Model that includes the competitive forces (i.e. suppliers, potential entrants, substitutes and buyers) facing the e-organization during the strategic planning phase. Also, managers should use his Value Chain model as a strategic planning tool (McNurlin and Sprague 2002).

Table 2.2 Meeting the Challenge of High-Velocity Change

Strategic posture	Actions	Strategy
Reacting to change	Introduce better products in response to new offerings of rivals	Be agile and respond as needed Defend and protect the firm's position
Anticipating change	Monitor new technological developments closely to predict future path	Pan ahead for expected future changes
Leading change	Introduce innovative products that open new markets and sput creation of whole new industries	Be a change agent and pace setter Influence the rules of the game Force the rivals to follow

Source: (Thompson and Strickland 2001)

REFERENCES

Albach, H., Meffert, H., et al. (2014). *Management of Permanent Change.* Wiesbaden: Springer Gabler.

Al-Debei, M. M., El-Haddadeh, R., & Avison, D. (2008a). *Defining the Business Model in the New World of Digital Business.* Proceedings of the 14th Americas Conference on Information Systems (AMCIS '08), Toronto, Canada, August 14–17.

Al-Debei, M. M., El-Haddadeh, R., & Avison, D. (2008b). *Towards a Business Model for Cellular Network and Telecommunication Operators: A Theoretical Framework.* Proceedings of the 13th Conference of the UK Academy for Information Systems, Bournemouth, UK, April 11–12.

Amit, R., & Zott, C. (2001). Value Creation in E-Business. *Strategic Management Journal, 22*(6–7), 493–520.

Anderson, D. M. (1997). *Agile Product Development for Mass Customization.* Chicago: Irwin.

Bakos, J. Y. (1997). Reducing Buyer Search Costs: Implications for Electronic Marketplaces. *Management Science, 43*(12), 1676–1692.

Ball, D. A., McCulloch, W. H., Jr., Frantz, P. L., Geringer, J. M., & Mirror, M. S. (2004). *International Business: The Challenge of Global Competition.* Boston, MA: McGraw-Hill.

Berger, R. (2014). *Unternehmenstransformation.* Retrieved April, 2015, from http://www.rolandberger.de/media/pdf/rb_press/RB_feature_corporate_transformation_g_20040820.pdf.

Bouwman, H. (2002). *The Sense and Nonsense of Business Models.* International Workshop on Business Models, HEC Lausanne, 6 p. cat. O, Projectcode: ICT.

Brynjolfsson, E., & Smith, M. D. (2000). Frictionless Commerce? A Comparison of Internet and Conventional Retailers. *Management Science, 46,* 563–585.

Bulik, B. S. (2000). Survival of the Fattest. *Business, 2.0*(July 11), 184–187.

Business Week. (2000). Americans See the New Economy All Around Them. *Business Week,* May 19.

Campanovo, G., & Pigneur, Y. (2003). *Business Model Analysis Applied to Mobile Business.* Proceedings of the 5th International Conference on Enterprise Information Systems, April 23–26, Angers.

Chan, R. Y., & Wong, Y. H. (1999). Bank Generic Strategies: Does Porter's Theory Apply in an International Banking Center. *International Business Review, 8,* 561–590. Retrieved November 11, 2014, from http://oapen.org/search?identifier=560292.

Clay, K., Krishnan, R., Wolff, E., & Fernandes, D. (2002). Retail Strategies on the Web: Price and Non-Price Competition in the Online Book Industry. *The Journal of Industrial Economics, 50*(3), 351–367.

Consulting, S. T. (2014). *Chancen und herausforderungen durch digitale transformation*. Retrieved April, 2015, from http://www.strategy-transformation.com/digitale-transformation-verstehen/.

Cross, R., & Smith, J. (1996). Customer-Focused Strategies and Tactics: Interactive Marketing Weighs in for Customers. In E. Forrest & R. Mizerski (Eds.), *Interactive Marketing: The Future Present* (pp. 5–28). Lincolnwood, IL: NTC Business Books.

Cuffe, S. S. (2005). Emerging Management Support Systems Models for Global Managers in the New Economy. *Journal of Knowledge Management Practice, 6*.

Dickson, G. W., & DeSanctis. (2001). *Information Techonology and the Future Enterprise: New Models for Managers*. Upper Saddle River, NJ: Prentice Hall.

Doppler, K., & Lauterburg, C. (2005). *Change Management: Den Unternehmenswandel gestalten*. Frankfurt: Campus Verlag.

Dornbusch, R. (2000). World Economic Trends. *MIT, 2*.

Dyer, J. H. (1997). Effective Interfirm Collaboration: How Firms Minimize Transaction Costs and Maximize Transaction Value. *Strategic Management Journal, 18*(7), 535–556.

Engel, C. (1999). The Internet and the Nation State. *Lectiones Jenenses, 21*.

Evans, P., & Wurster, T. S. (1999). *Blown to Bits: How the New Economics of Information Transforms Strategy*. Boston: Harvard Business School Publishing.

Glover, S. M., Liddle, S. W., & Prawitt, D. F. (2001). *E-Business Principles and Strategies for Accountants*. Upper Saddle River, NJ: Prentice Hall.

Gordijn, J., Ostenwalder, A., & Piguer, Y. (2005). Comparing Two Business Model Ontologies for Designing E-Business Models and Value Constellations. In *18th BLED Conference*, Bled, Slovenia, June 6–8.

Greenwood, J., & Jovanovic, B. (1999). The IT Revolution and the Stock Market. *American Economic Review, Papers and Proceedings*.

Griffith, V. (1999). Branding.com: How Brick-and-Mortar Companies Can Make It on the Internet. *Strategy and Business, 15*, 54–59.

Haaker, T., Faber, E., and Bouwman, H. (2004). *Balancing Strategic Interests and Technological Requirements for Mobile Services*. Proceedings of 6th International Conference on E-commerce, ICEC04, Delft, The Netherlands.

Haaker, T., Faber, E., & Bouwman, H. (2006). Balancing Customer and Network Value in Business Models for Mobile Services. *International Journal of Mobile Communication, 4*, 6.

Head, M., Archer, N., & Yuan, Y. (2000). World Wide Web Navigation Aid. *International Journal of Human-Computer Studies, 53*(2), 301–330.

Hitt, M. A., Ireland, R. D., & Hoskisson, R. E. (2001). *Strategic Management: Competitiveness and Globalization* (4th ed.). Cincinnati: South-Western.

Jalava, J., & Pohjola, M. (2008). The Roles of Electricity and ICT in Economic Growth: Case Finland. *Explorations in Economic History, 45*(3), 270–287.

Jorgenson, D. W. (2001). Information Technology and the US Economy. *American Economic Review, 91*(1), 1–32.

Kim, B. (2000). *E-Business Myths and Traps.* Seoul: LG Economic Institute.

Kubrick, K. (2013). *Introducing the dStrategy Digital Maturity Model.* DOI: http://www.digitalstrategyconference.com/blog/digital-strategy/introducingdstrategy-digital-maturity-model.

Leem, C. S., Suh, H. S., & Kim, D. S. (2004). A Classification of Mobile Business Models and Its Applications. *Industrial Management and Data Systems, 104*(1), 78–87.

Lucas, H. C., Agarwal, R., Clemons, E. K., El Sawy, O. A., & Weber, B. (2013). Impactful Research on Transformational Information Technology: An Opportunity to Inform New Audiences. *MIS Quaterly, 37*(2), 371–382.

Magretta, J. (1998). The Power of Virtual Integration: An Interview with Dell Computer's Michael Dell. *Harvard Business Review, 76*(2), 73–84.

Magretta, J. (2002). Why Business Models Matter. *Harvard Business Review, 80*(5), 86–92.

McGrath, R. G. (2010). Business Models: A Discovery Driven Approach. *Long Range Planning, 43*(2–3), 247–261.

McKnight, L. W., & Bailey, J. P. (1995). *An Introduction into Internet Economics.* Retrieved March 3, 2018, from http://www.press.umich.edu/jep/works/McKniIntro.html.

McNurlin, B. C., & Sprague, R. H., Jr. (2002). *Information Systems Management in Practice* (5th ed.). Upper Saddle River, NJ: Prentice Hall.

Merrilees, B. (2001). Do Traditional Strategic Concepts Apply in the E-Marketing Context? *Journal of Business Strategies, 18*, 177–190.

Miller, D. (1988). Relating Porter's Business Strategies to Environment and Structure: Analysis and Performance Implications. *Academy of Management Journal, 31*, 280–308.

Miller, D. (1991). Generalists and Specialists: Two Business Strategies and Their Contexts. *Advances in Strategic Management, 7*, 3–41.

Miller, D., & Friesen, P. (1986). Porter's Generic Strategies and Performance: An Empirical Examination with American Data. *Organizational Science, 7*, 37–55.

Modahl, M. (2000). *Now or Never: How Companies Must Change Today to Win the Battle for Internet Consumers.* New York: HarperBusiness.

Morris, M., Schindehutte, M., & Allen, J. (2005). The Entrepreneur's Business Model: Toward a Unified Perspective. *Journal of Business Research, 58*(6), 726–735.

OECD. (1999). *The Knowledge-Based Economy. Organisation for Economic Co-Operation and Development.* Paris.

Osterwalder, A. (2005). Clarifying Business Models: Origins, Present, and Future of the Concept. *Communications of the AIS, 15*(May), 2–40.

Petrovic, O., Kittl, C., & Teksten, D. (2001). *Developing Business Models for eBusiness.* Proceedings of the International conference on Electronic Commerce.

Phan Doan Nam. (1998). *Cong San Magazine,* 15.

Pine, J. (1993). *Mass Customization: The New Frontier in Business Competition.* Boston: Harvard Business School Press.

Porter, M. E. (1980). *Competitive Strategy: Techniques for Analyzing Industries and Competitors.* New York: Free Press.

Porter, M. E. (2001). Strategy and the Internet. *Harvard Business Review,* 79(2), 62–78.

Quah, D. T. (1999). The Weightless Economy in Growth. *The Business Economist,* 30(1), 40–53.

Rajala, R., & Westerlund, M. (2005). Business Models: A New Perspective on Knowledge-Intensive Services in the Software Industry. 18th Bled eCommerce Conference eIntegration in Action, Bled, Slovenia, 1–15.

Rossman, A., Steimel, K., & Wichmann, S. (2014). Digital Transformation Report. Neuland GmbH. Retrieved October 2, 2018, from https://www.wiwo.de/downloads/10773004/1/DTA_Report_neu.pdf.

Shapiro, C., & Varian, R. H. (1998). *Information Rules: A Strategic Guide for the Network Economy.* Cambridge, MA: Harvard Business School Press.

Shepard, S. B. (1997). The New Economy: What It Really Means. *Business Week,* November 17.

Stähler, P. (2002, October). Business Models as an Unit of Analysis for Strategizing. *International Workshop on Business Models, Lausanne, Switzerland,* 45(7), 2990–2995.

Thompson, A. A., & Strickland, A. J., III. (2001). *Strategic Management* (12th ed.). Boston, MA: McGraw-Hill.

Tikkanen, H., Lamberg, J. A., Parvinen, P., & Kallunki, J. P. (2005). Managerial Cognition, Action and the Business Model of the Firm. *Management Decision,* 43(6), 789–809.

Timmers, P. (1998). Business Models for Electronic Markets. *Electronic Markets,* 8(2), 3–8.

Uhlenbruck, K., Hitt, M., & Semadeni, M. (2001). Corporate Strategy in the New Economy: Outcomes of Four Types of Acquisitions. Presented at the Annual Meeting of the Strategic Management Society. San Francisco, CA. *Innovation Research.* USA: Fox School of Bus.

Varian, H. R. (1998). *Markets for Information Goods.* Retrieved October 22, 2017, from http://people.ischool.berkeley.edu/~hal/Papers/japan/japan.html.

Westerman, G., Calméjane, C., Bonnet, D., Ferraris, P., & McAfee, A. (2011). Digital transformation: A roadmap for billion-dollar organizations. *MIT Center for Digital Business and Capgemini Consulting,* 1, 1–68.

Williamson, O. E. (1983). Organizational Innovation: The Transaction Cost Approach. In J. Ronen (Ed.), *Entrepreneurship* (pp. 101–133). Lexington, MA: Lexington Books.

Wolff, R. (2001). The New Wealth of Nations. *The Economist.* Retrieved October, 2018, from https://www.economist.com/special-report/2001/06/14/the-new-wealth-of-nations.

Xiong, C. (2003). Online Stores Try New Pitch: Fetch It Yourself. *The Wall Street Journal,* November 19: D1, D4.

Yang, Z., & Jun, M. (2002). Consumer Perception of E-Service Quality: From Internet Purchaser and Non-Purchaser Perspectives. *Journal of Business Strategies, 19*(1), 19.

Yelkur, R., & DaCosta, M. M. N. (2001). Differential pricing and segmentation on the internet: The case of hotels. *Management Decision, 15,* 40–50.

Yoffie, D. B., & Cusumano, M. (1999). Judo Strategy: The Competitive Dynamics of Internet Time. *Harvard Business Review, 77*(1), 71–81.

Zahn, E., Foschiani, S., et al. (2000). Wissen und Strategiekompetenz als Basis für die Wettbewerbsfähigkeit von Unternehmen. In P. Hammann & J. Freiling (Eds.), *Die Ressourcen-und Kompetenzperspektive des Strategischen Managements* (pp. 47–68). Deutscher Universitätsverlag.

Zettlemeyer, F. (1996). *The Strategic Use of Consumer Search Cost.* Unpublished Ph.D. Thesis, Institute of Technology, Massachusetts.

Zott, C., & Amit, R. (2010). Designing Your Future Business Model: An Activity System Perspective. *Long Range Planning, 43,* 216–226.

CHAPTER 3

Digital Transformation Business Landscape

The background and basic understanding of digital transformation; its benefits, the two perspectives of digital transformation, the four dimensions of digital transformation strategies and the procedural aspects of digital transformation strategies are discussed.

Following that, there is an explanation on how to integrate digital transformation into firms and some challenges and strategic paths in order to do this effectively.

In the previous chapters we show how the fourth industrial revolution promotes changes and a point of inflection in the conception of the traditional economic system and, consequently, the emergence of new business models. These irrefutable facts derive in deep and horizontal changes in the company the "Digital Transformation". A concept—coined by McKinsey—that represents the challenges that a company must face before the comsumer's digital revolution. Therefore, it is a paradigm shift that profoundly affects the company but is proportionally related to the evolution of the new 100% digital consumer.

It is for this reason, as it could not be otherwise, that in this chapter the concept of Digital Transformation is approached from a strategic perspective; the benefits, dimensions, elements and success patterns of Digital Transformation strategies, procedural aspects and responsabilities, the integration of the Digital Transformation strategis into firms, the challenges and the paths (phases, integration and metrics) that make up the roadamap to carry out this transformation.

© The Author(s), under exclusive license to Springer Nature Switzerland AG 2020
A. Landeta Echeberria, *A Digital Framework for Industry 4.0*,
https://doi.org/10.1007/978-3-030-60049-5_3

1   BACKGROUND AND BASIC UNDERSTANDING

In the current context characterized by profound changes, as we will discuss later in the present Chapter, the organizational transformation in all firms—among other factors—the organizational transformation will be present throughout of the whole process of change (definition of new business lines based on the application of ICT or/and in the redefinition of traditional business lines) at different levels.

In this framework, organizational transformation is defined as simultaneous major changes in key activity domains (e.g. strategy, structure and power distribution) that typically occur over a brief interval of time (Wischnevsky and Damanpour 2006). It is also a complex, revolutionary and continuous process that demands fundamental changes in the organizational structures and systems through product development and service delivery (Romanelli and Tushman 1994). Such a transformation may lead to the reassessment of organisational norms and values as well as a change of service delivery systems. Hence, the transformation process itself becomes complex and chaotic in its nature and might indeed produce a radical departure from the current state. Accordingly, organisational transformation can have a major structural and fundamental impact on an entire organization.

Therefore, it must be accepted that since technologies can trigger such changes and provide the means for moving out of the past toward a more efficient and powerful future, organisations are increasingly expected to incorporate digital technology into their business practices to improve competitiveness (Henderson and Venkatraman 1993). In this regard, Digital Transformation can be defined as an organizational transformation that integrates digital technologies and business processes in a digital economy. Yet DT is much more than mere process redesign. It is about structuring new business operations to facilitate and fully leverage firms' core competence through digital technology in order to attain competitive advantage (Brynjolfsson and Hitt 2000). Therefore, it is critical to understand precisely how organizations manage their transformation to capitalize upon the benefits of digital technologies.

Based on the literature review, two views reveal a firm's:

1. Digital Transformations strategically fit with its resources and capabilities can engender the firm's competitive advantage (Barney 1991); and

2. Competitive advantages derive from the better use of its resources, rather than better resources (Mahoney and Pandian 1992).

In this respect, Wipro Digital, the digital business unit of Wipro Limited, released in May 2017 a study commissioned an online survey of 400 senior-level executives in the United States with more than 100 employees that indicates leadership within Digital Transformation may be in crisis. Half of senior executives polled across companies feel that their company is not successfully executing against 50% of their strategies. The study surveyed 400 senior-level US executives about the Digital Transformation strategies within their organizations.

The study's findings also show that while 91% of executives are aligned on what Digital Transformation means, only 4% realize half of their digital investment in under one year—with the majority of respondents saying it has taken their company 2–3 years to see at least half of these investments come to fruition.

In the same way, "Digital Transformation efforts are coming up short on intended ROI, in part because Digital Transformation is as much a leadership issue as it is a strategy, technology, culture, and talent issue", says Rajan Kohli, Senior Vice President and Global Head, Wipro Digital. And, likewise, "real Digital Transformation occurs when courageous leaders align goals in practice as well as theory, manage opportunity more than risk, and prioritize the future vs. retrofit the present".

Correspondingly, in the present study, the authors refer to following key study findings, identifying leadership issues as a key factor in the widespread stall in Digital Transformation efforts:

1. **Companies are aligned on what Digital Transformation means in theory, but not in practice:** 91% of executives believe their company is aligned on the definition of Digital Transformation—yet 1 in 4 executives note that a key obstacle to success in their strategies was a lack of alignment on what Digital Transformation actually means. Lack of a clear transformation strategy was similarly cited by 35% of executives as a key barrier to achieving its full digital potential.
2. **Underlying doubts among leaders:** Nearly 1 in 5 senior executives admit that they secretly believe that Digital Transformation projects in their company are a waste of time.
3. **Leadership mindset & skills challenges:** CEOs, CTOs and CIOs are almost equally likely to serve as the primary driver for Digital

Transformation strategies, and they are at least twice as likely to do so more than any other senior executive—yet mindset and skill challenges, such as resistance to introducing new ways of working (39%), and feeling overwhelmed by digital complexity (40%), were cited as the top two leading obstacles preventing a company from achieving its full digital potential.

4. **Focus on back-end benefits vs. product innovation and growth:** Back-end departments such as Operations and IT are by far the leading beneficiaries of Digital Transformation strategies, and combined with Procurement and Finance, are cited by 60% of executives as reaping the benefits. Far less likely to benefit are departments such as Product Development (15%), Marketing (13%), and Sales (10).

5. **IT investment by executive versus ownership:** CMOs are spending more than ever on IT—yet they are the least likely of any senior executive (2%) to drive Digital Transformation strategies. Chief Digital Officers fare little better in driving just 12%. Findings correlate with the fact that nearly 1 in 4 executives say that a key obstacle to success is that their company's structure hasn't changed to reflect digital imperatives.

In essence, we want to draw attention to the importance of Digital Transformation and its strategy framework for further successful implementation within any kind of firms. Bearing in mind that at the moment there is not much scientific literature on the subject and, in most cases, we are forced to take inspiration from reports from ICT consultancies.

Thus, in order to understand the phenomenon object of study, we will base ourselves on the study prepared by i-Scoop "Digital Transformation: The online guide to digital business transformation"[1] (n.d.). As, it takes account of an accurate definition and strategy framework of Digital Transformation.

Digital Transformation is the profound transformation of business and organizational activities, processes, competencies and models to fully leverage the changes and opportunities of a mix of digital technologies and their accelerating impact across society in a strategic and prioritized way, with present and future shifts in mind.

---

[1] Availble from https://www.i-scoop.eu/digital-transformation/.

While Digital Transformation is predominantly used in a business context, it also impacts other organizations such as governments, public sector agencies and organizations which are involved in tackling societal challenges such as pollution and aging populations by leveraging one or more of these existing and emerging technologies. In some countries, such as Japan, Digital Transformation even aims to impact all aspects of life with the country's Society 5.0 initiative, which goes far beyond the limited Industry 4.0 vision in other countries.

In this respect, digital maturity frameworks and benchmarks do have value. They indicate that Digital Transformation is a journey towards acquiring a set of capabilities and changing a range of processes, functions, models and more with the purpose to (be able to) leverage the changes and opportunities of digital technologies and their impact across society in a strategic and prioritized way, as we defined Digital Transformation earlier.

This comes with several consequences according to the i-Scoop study mentioned above:

Digital Transformation is not just about a specific project, process or optimization exercise. It's a holistic given and it doesn't happen overnight. There are many components and intermediate goals. It happens in incremental steps, hence the digital maturity views.

- The various stages, steps, projects and so on in the context of Digital Transformation have one or more goals as such, yet at the same time fit within the broader purposewhich we just established by referring to (part of) our definition. In other words: you have a roadmap and an end goal in mind.
- Although it might sound like a contradiction in terminis, the end goal of Digital Transformation changes, making it a journey. New technologies will offer new opportunities and challenges, as will changing market conditions, competitive landscapes and so forth. While Digital Transformation has a goal of preparing us for those, at the same time that goal as such is subject to change.
- Change is a constant. From a Digital Transformation strategy perspective this means that uncertainties, risks and changes are factored into each incremental step and the broader objectives but it also means that a Digital Transformation strategy comes with agile possibilities to change course, thanks to intermediate checks and balances

and a 'hyperaware' ability of continuous improvement or change (both are not the same).

Similarly, the report based on Global Executive Study and Research Project (2013). Digital Transformation's report "Embracing Digital Technology. A New Strategic Imperative"[2] by MIT Sloan Management Review and Capgemini Consulting finds that companies now face a digital imperative: adopt new technologies effectively or face competitive obsolescence.

This report, as well as the survey,[3] focuses on Digital Transformation, which we define as the use of new digital technologies (social media, mobile, analytics or embedded devices) to enable major business improvements, such as enhancing customer experience, streamlining operations or creating new business models.

The key findings from the survey are as follows:

- According to 78% of respondents, achieving Digital Transformation will become critical to their organizations within the next two years.
- However, 63% said the pace of technology change in their organization is too slow.
- The most frequently cited obstacle to Digital Transformation was "lack of urgency."
- Only 38% of respondents said that Digital Transformation was a permanent fixture on their CEO's agenda.
- Where CEOs have shared their vision for Digital Transformation, 93% of employees feel that it is the right thing for the organization. But, a mere 36% of CEOs have shared such a vision.

1.1   The Benefits of Digital Transformation

In the same report,[4] the benefits of Digital Transformation are analyzed, as follows.

Companies that effectively manage digital technology can expect to gain in one or more of three areas: better customer experiences and

---

[2] Available from https://sloanreview.mit.edu/projects/embracing-digital-technology/.
[3] Survey available from https://sloanreview.mit.edu/projects/embracing-digitaltechnology/.
[4] Available also from https://aaltodoc.aalto.fi/handle/123456789/16540.

engagement, streamlined operations and new lines of business or business models. Though innovative new business models are what every CEO dreams of, companies more often see digital technologies help transform their customer experience or operations. Business model transformation is difficult, and farless prevalent, according to survey respondents.

- **Customer experiences reflect the clearest impact of Digital Transformation.** The survey found that improving customer relationships was the area where companies were having the most success with digital technology. Most prominent was improving the overall customer experience, followed closely by enhancing products and services in customer-friendly ways.
- **Survey respondents said their organizations also are seeing improvements in operations, in part in automating operations.** A number or respondents said internal communications are sharply improved, especially through using social media. For example, Jon Bidwell (as cited in Fitzgerald et al. 2013), chief innovation officer at Chubb, a large specialty insurer, told us that social business tools and processes had transformed the company's innovation culture, helping it develop products and understand risks as rapidly as new markets emerged.
- **The opportunity for digital technologies to create new businesses is real, and a quarter of respondents expect Digital Transformation to launch new products and services.** General Electric is pushing an Internet of Things service strategy that will help it tell customers how to schedule maintenance and avoid part failures, improving operations. The company expects it will sell services related to maintaining its products.
- **Of course, more efficient products may well reduce demand for new GE goods.** But William Ruh (as cited in Fitzgerald et al. 2013), vice president of software at General Electric, notes "there's upside for us in the services. We can grow on the services side, and they're winning and we're winning."
- **But business model transformation is also elusive.** A mere 7% of respondents said that their company's digital initiatives were helping to launch new businesses, and only 15% said new business models were emerging thanks to digital technology.
- **It could be that these technologies are so new that they simply haven't had time to be turned into new business opportunities.**

One respondent noted that in his company, "the belief is that digital technologies are not that effective yet in our marketplace." Another said customers weren't ready for new models yet, because they are "highly conservative and resistant to change."

In addition, we must take into account the analysis of the concept "Digital Transformation" from two different perspectives, as mentioned below.

1.2   Two Perspectives of Digital Transformation

The main references can be done to work of (Matt et al. 2015). These authors consider that in recent years, firms in almost all industries have conducted a number of initiatives[5] to explore new digital technologies and to exploit their benefits. This frequently involves transformations of key business operations and affects products and processes, as well as organizational structures and management concepts. Companies need to establish management practices to govern these complex transformations.

In this respect, the same authors put emphasis on; the Digital Transformation strategies take on a different perspective and pursue different goals. Coming from a business centric perspective, these strategies focus on the transformation of products, processes, and organizational aspects owing to new technologies. Their scope is more broadly designed and explicitly includes digital activities at the interface with or fully on the side of customers, such as digital technologies as part of end-user products. This con-stitutes a clear difference to process automation and optimization, since Digital Transformation strategies go beyond the process paradigm, and include changes to and implications for products, services, and business models as a whole (Fig. 3.1).

Similar to the previous discussion on the alignment between business strategies and IT strategies (Henderson and Venkatraman 1993), it is critical to obtain a close fit between Digital Transformation strategies, IT strategies, and all other organizational and functional strategies. Research has addressed this issue and has sought to consolidate IT strategies and business strategies into a comprehensive "digital business strategy" (Bharadwaj et al. 2013).

---

[5]All initiatives availble from https://www.plattform-i40.de/I40/Redaktion/EN/Downloads/Publikation/industrie-40-in-a-global-context.pdf?__blob=publicationFile&v=1.

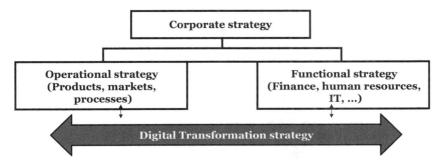

Fig. 3.1   Relation between digital transformation strategy and other corporate strategies. (Source: Matt et al. 2015)

2   THE 4 DIMENSIONS OF DIGITAL TRANSFORMATION STRATEGIES

The same authors distingues between, independent of the industry or firm, Digital Transformation strategies have certain elements in common. These elements can be ascribed to four essential dimensions: *use of technologies, changes in value creation, structural changes,* and *financial aspects.* The *use of technologies* addresses a company's attitude towards new technologies as well as its ability to exploit these technologies.

From a business perspective, the use of new technologies often implies *changes in value creation.* These concern the impact of Digital Transformation strategies on firms' value chains, that is how far the new digital activities deviate from the classical—often still analog—core business. Further deviations offer opportunities to expand and enrich the current products and services portfolio, but they are often accompanied by a stronger need for different technological and product-related competences and higher risks owing to lwss experience in the new field.

The digitization of products or services can enable or require different forms of monetization, or even adjustments to firms' business scope, if other markets or new customer segments are addressed. With different technologies in use and different forms of value creation, *structural changes* are often needed to provide an adequate basis for the new operations.

For this assessment it is further important, whether it is mainly products, processes, or skills that are affected most by these changes. If the
extent of the changes is fairly limited, it might be more reasonable to
integrate the new operations into existing corporate structures, while for
more substantial changes it might be better to create a separate subsidiary
within the firm. However, the former three dimensions can only be transformed after considering *financial aspects*. These include a firm's urgency
to act owing to a diminishing core business and its ability to finance a
Digital Transformation endeavor; financial aspects are both a driver and a
bounding force for the transformation. While lower financial pressure on
the core business may reduce the perceived urgency to act, companies
already under financial pressure might lack external ways to finance a
transformation.

To ensure the successful rollout of a Digital Transformation strategy
and fully exploit its intended effects, it is essential to closely align the four
different dimensions: use of technologies, changes in value creation, structural changes, and financial aspects. The four transformational dimensions
and their dependencies can be integrated into one joint Digital
Transformation Framework (Fig. 3.2).

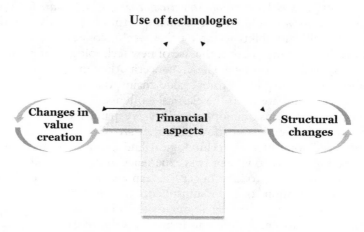

Fig. 3.2 Digital transformation framework: balancing four transformational
dimensions. (Source: Matt et al. 2015)

2.1 Procedural Aspects of Digital Transformation Strategies

Therefore, (Matt et al. 2015) claimed that Digital Transformation is a continuous complex undertaking that can substantially shape a company and its operations. It is therefore important to assign adequate and clear responsabilities for the definition and implementation of a Digital Transformation strategy.

To date, there is no clear answer to which senior manager should be in charge of a Digital Transformation strategy. In addition to CIOs or even CEOs, potential candidates include dedicated business transformation managers or the fairly new role of the Chief Digital Officer (CDO). In any case, given the long duration of many transformational processes, this should preferably continue to be one and the same person.

Further, beginning with the initial planning phase, top management support is essential along the whole transformation process, since Digital Transformation strategies affect the entire company, and their execution may therefore result in resistance from different areas of the company. To deal with such resistance, transformation leadership skills are essential and require the active involvement of the different stakeholders affected by the transformation.

Besides adequate staffing for both the initial phase and further implementation, firms need to find procedures for formulating, implementing, evaluating, and—if necessary—adapting Digital Transformation strategies.

2.2 Integrating Digital Transformation into Firms

MIT Center for Digital Business and Capgemini Consulting's study (multi-year study is an exploratory investigation involving 157 executive-level interviews in 50 companies in 15 countries)[6]: Digital Transformation: a roadmap for billion-dollar organizations states that

- Analysis of the interviews shows clear patterns. Executives are digitally transforming three key areas of their enterprises: customer experience, operational processes and business models.

---

[6] Available from https://sloanreview.mit.edu/article/the-nine-elements-of-digital-ttransformation/.

Within each of the three pillars, different elements are changing. These nine elements form a set of building blocks for Digital Transformation. Currently, no company in our sample has fully transformed all nine elements. Rather, executives are selecting among these building blocks to move forward in the manner that they believe is right for their organizations. The tenth element—digital capabilities—is an essential enabler for transformations in all areas.

3   Challenges and Strategic Paths to Transformation

What is causing firms to have difficulty starting or benefiting from Digital Transformation? Challenges occur in all three elements of the transformation process: Initiation, Execution and Coordination.

In summary, the challenges identified in the aforementioned study[7] present the following classification (Fig. 3.3):

3.1   Main Characteristics of Transformation Process Elements

Initiation challenges (lack of impetus, regulation and reputation, unclear business case);

- Lack of impetus
  - Impetus often starts at the very top of the firm. Executives are justifiably skeptical of the benefits of emerging technologies. The experience of e-commerce taught many executives that a fast follower approach could sometimes be lower risk than a pioneering approach. However, this skepticism can result in bureaucratic investment processes that prevent the firm from engaging in useful digitally enabled experiments and business changes.
  - Company performance can also slow the move to transformation. If the company is not experiencing pain, the perceived risk of change may outweigh the potential benefits in the minds of many executives.

---

[7] Available also from Pham&Roubi_Antoine&Juliette_Digital maturity and value creation.pdf.

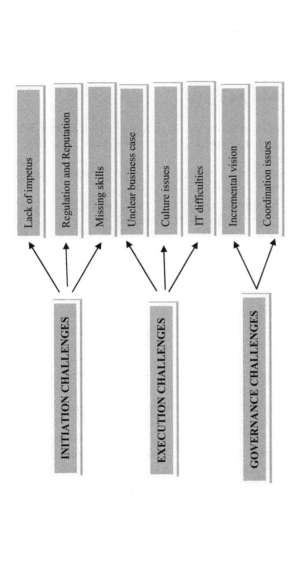

Fig. 3.3 Elements of the transformation process: initiation, execution and coordination. (Source: Author's own elaboration from Digital Transformation: a roadmap for billion-dollar organizations study 2011)

- And other concern issue can be lack of awareness of the opportunities or threats of Digital Transformation.
- Executives need not be aware of all changes in industries outside their own, but knowing major digital consumer services products such as Tripadvisor, Facebook or eBay can be very useful fodder for envisioning how executives might change their own businesses.

• Regulation and reputation

Many executives, especially in healthcare and financial services, are being careful about mobile and social technologies because of security and privacy concerns.

This has reputational repercussions well beyond any regulatory penalties.

Companies, especially in financial services, are taking a slow approach to social media for fear of regulatory sanction.

While these regulatory concerns are real, they need not prevent companies from moving forward.

• Unclear business case

Healthy skepticism or regulatory concerns are legitimate reasons to be careful when investigating new technologies. Certainly not all digital initiatives make sense for all companies (or for all employees in the company).

Some initiatives can be justified in the traditional way, through quantified economic business cases. Audio and videoconferencing technologies, for example, can be justified on travel cost savings or other efficiencies, as could a financial firm's move to a transformed office environment.

Larger process transformations also can cite clear returns, such as when an apparel firm justified its move to digital design processes through cost savings and significantly shortened product development cycles.

However, as with many innovations, Digital Transformation investments often have less clear business cases than these examples. Many companies considered their initial forays into Facebook or Twitter as simple experiments built with limited funding and risk investigating the potential of the new media.

Other initiatives are funded as strategic foundation investments that build infrastructure and capabilities to be used elsewhere. These investments rarely go through the rigor of developing a quantified business case, but rather are undertaken as strategic bets.

Similarly, several firms hired senior executives or content experts to get started in the analytics and social media spaces. The new leaders must financially justify their existence in the future, but the initial investment was considered as capability building.

The real value of Digital Transformation comes not from the initial investment, but from continuously re-envisioning how capabilities can be extended with digital technology to increase revenue, cut costs or gain other benefits. Initial investments, made with or without a financial business case, become foundational capabilities on which additional investments can be made.

Execution challenges (missing skills, culture issues, IT difficulties);

While a top-level impetus for transformation is important, it is often not enough. While a top-level impetus for transformation is important, it is often not enough. Interviewees cited three missing elements that threatened to prevent them from moving forward successfully.

- Missing skills

Analytic-based decision-making does not always come naturally to people accustomed to using "professional judgment" or other methods to make decisions.

Firms are filling gaps by hiring experts or working with vendors. Skills that are in short supply in one industry can sometimes be found in others.

Meanwhile, although the executive recognizes that smart embedded devices will be essential to the firm's future product strategy "We have nobody to look into that."

However, it is encountering knowledge integration issues, as key skills are located in different vendors.

- Culture issues

Cultural issues can also become a bottleneck for Digital Transformation. A major cultural issue is related to changes in jobs due to automationor information empowerment.

One lever for change is to hire new leaders. These people, while bringing new skills, also bring new vision that helps change the culture in their areas.

Labor relations issues are a stickier source of culture change issues.

* IT difficulties

Digital initiatives are built on a solid foundation of technology-enabled processes and data, as well as the analytics, solution delivery and relationship capabilities to create and extend that platform.

Information technology is a fundamental part of the firm's digital capabilities. However, many companies find their information technology infrastructures and capabilities severely lacking.

Beyond technical issues in IT, relationship issues can be difficult. A history of poor business/IT relations is a difficult foundation for the collaborative work required in Digital Transformation.

A strong IT/business relationship can be very helpful in transformation.

Governance challenges (incremental vision, coordination issues);

Benefiting from transformation typically requires changes in processes or decision-making that span traditional organizational or functional structures. Transformation, like any major organizational change, requires top-down effort to help employees envision a different reality, and coordination to ensure the firm moves in the right direction.

* Incremental vision

While incremental investments can be effective starting places to build digital capability, the largest benefits of Digital Transformation come from truly transforming activities. This requires a more radical vision—one that offers a view of a different way of working, not just a faster or more efficient one.

Unless senior executives establish a transformative vision of the future, managers in the rest of the firm will tend to locally optimize within their own spheres of authority.

An overarching vision can span organizational boundaries. Firms undergoing globalization are envisioning themselves as a single entity with local offices, rather than a collection of independent units.

Coordination Issues
Many firms fail to transform because of coordination difficulties across business units or processes. Units are able to make progress in their own areas, but are unable to influence practices in other units.

A further concern arises from coordination issues between new and traditional businesses or processes.
This channel conflict is real, and can be very painful for managers in traditional units that lose when new businesses gain. It often must be addressed through an overarching vision.

References

Barney, J. (1991). Firm Resources and Sustained Competitive Advantage. *Journal of Management, 17*(1), 99–117. Retrieved September, 2017, from Concept and Context of SHRM Chapter 1–5.docx.

Bharadwaj, A., El Sawy, O. A., Pavlou, P. A., & Venkatraman, N. (2013). Digital Business Strategy: Toward a Next Generation of Insights. *MIS Quarterly, 37*(2), 471–482.

Brynjolfsson, E., & Hitt, L. M. (2000). Beyond computation: Information technology, organizational transformation and business practices. *The Journal of Economic Perspectives, 14*(4), 23–48.

Fitzgerald, M., Kruschwitz, N., Bonnet, D., & Welch, M. (2013). Embracing Digital Technology: A New Strategic Imperative. *MIT Sloan Management Review* and Capgemini Consulting. Retrieved October, 2, 2018, from https://sloanreview.mit.edu/projects/embracing-digital-technology/.

Henderson, J. C., & Venkatraman, N. (1993). Strategic Alignment: Leveraging Information Technology for Transforming Organizations. *IBM System Journal, 32*(1), 472–484.

i-Scoop. (n.d.). *Digital Transformation Strategy: The Bridges to Build.* Retrieved January 15, 2018, from https://www.i-scoop.eu/digital-transformation/digital-transformation-strategy/.

Mahoney, J. T., & Pandian, J. R. (1992). The Resource-Based View within the Conversation of Strategic Management. *Strategic Management Journal, 13*(5), 363–380.

Matt, C., Hess, T., & Benlian, A. (2015). Digital Transformation Strategies. *Business & Information Systems Engineering, 57*(5), 339–343. Retrieved March, 2016, from http://dx.doi.org.ezp-02.lirn.net/10.1007/s12599-015-0401-5.

Romanelli, E., & Tushman, M. L. (1994). Organizational Transformation as Punctuated Equilibrium: An Empirical Test. *The Academy of Management Journal, 37*(5), 1141–1166.

Wischnevsky, J. D., & Damanpour, F. (2006). Organizational Transformation and Performance: An Examination of Three Perspectives. *Journal of Managerial Issues, 18*(1), 104–128.

CHAPTER 4

Digital Transformation Implementation Plan

This chapter presents the establishment of a digital transformation road-map—A Digital Transformation Implementation Plan; its phases of development, integration and measurement, respectively.

1   DIGITAL TRANSFORMATION ROADMAP

In order to develop the aforementioned roadmap, a series of measures must be established, to be developed in three different stages; phases of development, integration and measurement.

1.1   *Phases of Development*

According to (Solis 2013), Digital Transformation is indeed a journey, and with every journey comes the steps that move you along your way. A Principal Analyst of Altimeter Group's and author of "6 Levels of Digital Transformation Maturity", in an era of Digital Darwinism[1]—is required to assembled a series of actions that provide a blueprint for implementing a Digital Transformation Plan which are described briefly below.

---

[1] Digital Darwinism gives way to innovations that define not only the next steps for transformation and your organization's path to digital maturity, but also new philosophies, models, and processes that pave the way for a new genre of business.

© The Author(s), under exclusive license to Springer Nature   75
Switzerland AG 2020
A. Landeta Echeberria, *A Digital Framework for Industry 4.0*,
https://doi.org/10.1007/978-3-030-60049-5_4

Strategize: set the vision and the value to capture: a clear and dynamic road-map that lays out the path forward is required because of the complexity of technology and use cases, the required process and cultural change, and the investment needed to scale a strategy. This involves not only a business case (linking the corporate strategy to the business drivers and specific business objectives), but also an aspirational vision. In this phase, executives can show the value of a future-oriented approach and help the organization see its role in the Fourth Industrial Revolution environment.

A company-wide framework that drives the implementation is also recommended to ensure homogeneous execution across the production unit and sites, which might have different starting points in terms of performance and maturity.

The strategy phase should conclude with the creation of a company-wide roadmap, built in collaboration with the business units. Roadmaps are normally structured in waves, based on the complexity of the use cases to be implemented and the starting point of each business unit.

The same author points out, every business faces Digital Darwinism. Some companies are far along the Digital Transformation process, while others have yet to begin a formal transformation strategy. Either way, every business tracks itself according to key stages that help communicate waypoints and direction. Identifying what those stages are and what defines them is the purpose behind a new research-based maturity model, "The 6 Levels of Digital Transformation Maturity".[2] It organizes the key moments and milestones along the path of Digital Transformation to offer visibility and guidance to those change agents leading the way.

Through (Solis 2013) research, six key stages many organizations go through in their Digital Transformation have been identified.

In this context, six levels of Digital Transformation Maturity are established, as mentioned in the above table (1) that contains the six levels of Digital Transformation Maturity in a shallow way shown below (Table 4.1).

It is clear that for this author, that the maturation of Digital Transformation is constant; "This was just a cursory overview of the important stages a business faces as it digitally transforms. Even though each stage is representative of noteworthy Chapters in Digital Transformation, they are not absolute nor meant to convey a linear path, nor is any phase isolated unto itself. I have learned time and time again

---

[2] Available from   https://www.cognizant.com/whitepapers/the-six-stages-of-digital-transformationmaturity.pdf.

Table 4.1 6 Levels of digital transformation maturity

(1) Business as usual	Businesses ignore or are unaware of the risks and opportunities of Digital Darwinism and continue their course as planned.
	Additionally, the culture of the organization is mostly risk-averse, with investments and ideas that operate within established confines and generally discouragement of anything or anyone that suggests otherwise.
	While digital is not ignored, it is not used as a formal directive within a Digital Transformation approach.
	Organizations are still following technology-first roadmaps and processes that are years old.
	Other attributes that define businesses in this phase demonstrate a lack of understanding or infrastructure around digital. There is no mastery of what digital is and no formal understanding of its impact on customers, employees, and markets. As such, a vision for what's possible and a plan to work toward it are absent. Training, strategies, metrics and workflow initiatives around digital are, for the most part, ad hoc.
	Additionally, the overall CX is still managed by individual departments (silos), with fragmented processes and systems that do not connect the dots in sales, CRM, support or marketing. This is caused by a lack of "one" customer view across the organization.
	Marketing is still campaign-based across multiple social, digital, and traditional channels with little or no collaboration across different disciplines. Most of the time, strategies are rooted in conventional practices without taking into account new platforms and networks and how to leverage them differently.
	Data exists in separate caches for every channel, without any opportunity for cross- or omni-channel engagement throughout the customer lifecycle.

(continued)

Table 4.1 (continued)

(2) Test and learn	Companies are starting to get it in this phase, usually because someone in some department recognizes that things aren't working as is. Or they see other businesses doing things differently.
	As such, digital, mobile, social and all disruptive tech introduces new opportunities to test and learn internally and externally. Change agents take action, which isn't necessarily organized or centralized. This creates internal buzz and concern around change and amplifies the opportunity for chaos as rogue experiments occur in isolation without cross-functional collaboration.
	But champions are the believers, and they serve as the sparks for driving Digital Transformation. Previous failures or lacklustre investments help agents of change discover that early pilots and experiments in emergent channels enable them not only to learn, but also offer proof points for success. These early efforts can also serve as internal best practices and case studies for what's possible.
	Companies explore how to better understand the connected customer journey and start to invest in research or workshops that get executives and strategists out of their comfort zones. Customer journey mapping and even employee journey mapping unveil possibilities for next steps. For example, post workshops; investments in social, mobile, digital and content strategies are experimented within respective groups where we start to see early forms of cross-team sharing and collaboration between them.
	Now, the company, though still operating in silos, expands into new spaces led by individual groups or loosely defined "circles" to explore new possibilities for internal and external programmes. Additionally, these initial teams explore how to work outside their coverage areas to make greater impacts while also making the case for more support and resources.
	Customer data for each channel still exists in silos; however, focus begins on acquiring customer data through listening. This listening capability also informs much of the content strategy, with efforts to create more real time relevant content rather than relying solely on campaigns created by outside agencies.

(3) Systemize and strategize	Digital Transformation starts to trigger strategic investments in people, processes, and technology. The organization is getting smarter, with its change agents seeing the bigger picture and starting to work formally toward it. We start to see IT and marketing form a working or formal alliance to expedite investments and a supporting infrastructure for transformation.

The Test and Learn stage offered tastes of new possibilities. At this point, companies are investing in ways to learn more about where and how to make more formalized investments for greater impact. Programmes become more intentional, and we also start to see the early stages of uniformity taking shape.

Executive education is key in this stage to earn support for formal programmes.

Digital literacy now becomes a primary focus to help stakeholders become masters of these new domains (digital, mobile, social) and how to operate within them. Among transformation and each technology circle, innovation becomes an official focal point to identify new opportunities and potential disruption outside of the organization.

Teams seek to more formally optimize efforts and resources. To do so, an executive sponsor for Digital Transformation is sought after and a case is made to earn official support. This introduces leverage, structure, and overall executive attention. As such, the sponsor and change agents invest in formal working groups (taskforces) to test and learn through organized, cross-functional pilot programmes usually focused on the digital customer experience (DCX). The team also explores technology investments and partnerships to scale pilots and possibilities.

Improving the DCX becomes a driver for transformation since it is tied to business goals and outcomes. Here, companies get traction through notable, but still largely disparate, pilot programmes strewn across multiple functions.

Led by change agents, pilots still tend to focus largely on DCX and marketing. Usually, a deeper customer-journey mapping exercise is conducted to reveal additional opportunities and priorities for transformation. As the journey is studied, data is analysed and new consumer behaviour and preferences feed into redesigning the DCX. Asking, "What would my digital customer do, and how is it different than those who are more traditional?" helps focus priority areas and efforts. Understanding the digital customer also plays a significant part in expanding this work to include programmes, people, and processes to support new efforts.

Sales and support initiatives start to find their way into the mix. As change agents either operate in silos themselves or are "matrixed" into helping other departments with their pilots, the lack of formal unity becomes a real pain point as change agents push forward and solving for it becomes tenable.

Metrics overall start to mature across every programme to scrutinize and optimize investments. Data too becomes fundamental to informing everything from understanding connected customer journeys, preferences, behaviours, personal interests, and context to using customer-facing technology to optimize the experience.

New expertise in these areas becomes a mandate, with new roles and responsibilities joining existing departments or becoming part of the Digital Transformation team to improve research, recommendations, and progress.

At the same time, content and overall marketing strategies start to shift from multi-channel broadcast campaigns to targeted/real-time engagement (personalized) opportunities that also unite efforts and facilitate cross-functional collaboration in each network/channel.

(continued)

Table 4.1 (continued)

(4) Adapt or die	If a flag were raised over HQ, it would read, "Adapt or Die!" There's notable momentum at this point, and change is something that the entire organization is starting to recognize and appreciate.

Businesses in this stage are becoming resilient. Efforts in Digital Transformation become intentional with short- and long-term goals/outcomes supported by investments in infrastructure. In fact, efforts are now more ambitious and organized formally, moving beyond prioritized-but-focused pilots to official pilots that span every category affecting the DCX and beyond. These include sales, service/support, and marketing, of course, but also start to expand into HR, product development, manufacturing, etc. Additionally, categories are formed under each, where common resources are shared across once-disparate departments, including:

- Data
- CRM
- Content
- Education and Training
- Governance

Investments in people, processes, and technology are formalized to optimize existing or new touch points in the digital customer journey. Efforts shift the traditional sales/marketing/commerce funnel focus to a more dynamic model that adapts with changes in technology and behaviour. Content is optimized for each channel, and there are coordinated and automated efforts between paid, owned, and earned media.

Experts explore mass personalization and contextual programming to provide more effective engagement strategies across every touch point and channel.

New data investments help monitor performance and news areas of opportunity. Tools and data systems are integrated to create a single view of the customer across every interaction point.

(5) Transformed and transforming	Digital Transformation is now in the company's DNA, and it becomes constant.
	Along the way, these efforts have reshaped the enterprise, creating new models and operating standards affecting people, process, and technology by function and line of business at both the local and enterprise-wide level. The organization is operating in a more unified manner with Digital Transformation efforts led/managed by a governing body.
	Every function and business unit of the company is managing aspects of Digital Transformation locally and also enterprise-wide. IT and other key functions invest in dynamic architecture and sophisticated/mature technology to optimize the change process and empower new models to collaborate and adapt. This is done according to a renewed or cutting-edge vision and mission for this new stage.
	Leadership transcends this movement into the establishment of a new agenda around culture, purpose and the future.
	As other groups realize the impact of Digital Transformation, efforts are then expanded to transform the lifeline.
	Change agents become new leaders of the digital and physical CX.
	Marketing strategies shift beyond campaigns with an emphasis of investments made in on-going, day-to-day programmes, resources, platforms, metrics and data.
	Content is optimized for each channel and rooted in context to personalize engagement across devices based on their state and intent within the journey.
	A harmonious journey map with intent and attribution is created for each touch point. Innovation in strategy, execution, and measurement continues to push innovation forward in every facet that touches and supports everything around the customer and employee ecosystems.

(continued)

Table 4.1 (continued)

(6) Innovate or die	A culture of innovation becomes prevalent. Now, new models, roles, and investments shift focus toward innovation to accelerate transformation and identify new, unconventional opportunities for growth.
	The workgroup(s) once dedicated to transformation and technology shift focus toward innovation and disruption. They quickly evolve into the next "iterative" effort or the next stage in transformation to understand how to identify innovation and disruption outside of the organization. Innovation centres or teams are officially formed to recruit new talent, identify new technology and investment/acquisition opportunities, and learn where to focus transformation efforts over the short/long term.
	A flatter management and decisioning model rather than a traditional hierarchy supports the organization. Ideation and knowledge acquisition are part of everyone's everyday job. Executives and the teams/departments and individuals they manage are not only empowered to ideate; they are a measured part of performance at every level. This means that ideas are sourced, sorted, prioritized, and explored as part of the day-to-day management infrastructure. Employees are expected to contribute to progress, and managers are measured by their ability to identify and triage bona fide opportunities. Time is often allocated in the normal work Schedule to allot for learning or ideating. Additionally, higher education is offered to instil new expertise and keep employees in line with the needs of an evolving digital organization.
	To understand how innovation affects business and how to apply lessons internally, leadership embarks on guided tours of technology hotspots, such as Silicon Valley. In these cases, executives meet with companies leading the way for innovation, such as Twitter, Tesla, Facebook and Ideo, among others, to get a first-hand view of how and why they operate differently.
	In more advanced instances, innovation centres or teams are officially formed within the organization or moved to an innovation hub or hubs around the country/world. The objectives for these groups vary and often include:
	- Recruiting new talent
	- Identifying new technologies for internal piloting
	- Investing in or acquiring start ups
	- Surfacing new opportunities for products and service development
	Furthermore, many innovative companies are seeking to actively become contributors or members of these communities to further spotlight innovation to the community at large, as well as to the greater organization.
	This is done, for example, by hosting hackathons, start-up showcases, and conference-like programming to help entrepreneurs and business leaders learn from industry experts and thought leaders.
	Shifting toward innovation unlocks an entire different maturity model. Lessons learned here are applied in real time to improve internal and external operations, as well as market strategies in specific cases. As time passes and experience develops, insights are examined for greater impact across the organization.

Source: Author's own from (Solis 2013)

that organizations can and do occupy more than one stage at any one time. Digital's impact across the enterprise is vast. And transformation is only partly defined by technology. Its ultimate success is defined by the reworking of several key business functions, processes, and models, with the state of each contributing to the evolution of digital maturity. This includes governance, education and training, CX, employee engagement, data, marketing/content strategy, digital integration, and innovation. Combined, in any size and shape, investments in any or all of these fronts equate to Digital Transformation. Its extent and impact define placement on the maturity map, which demonstrates progress, orientation, and direction".

1.2   Integration

Regarding the strategic phase associated with the integration, (Matt et al. 2015) within the Digital Transformation strategies report i-Scoop "Digital Transformation strategy: the bridges to build"[3] (n/d) have recognized the potential of Digital Transformation strategy which in a synthetic way is presented below.

A Digital Transformation strategy starts with answering essential questions such as the what, why, how and who. A Digital Transformation strategy builds bridges between current state and desired long-term plan.

And as Digital Transformation by definition is holistic and requires integration and collaboration, a Digital Transformation strategy looks at building blocks and the bridges to connect them, as well as barriers and new bridges to overcome them.

In a business reality where 'the business', with a leading (yet, non-exclusive) role for marketing and the CMO, increasingly takes decisions on technology budgets, we see that it's often hard for IT and information management professionals, who are essential in Digital Transformation, to speak the language of the CMO or other business executives, which traditionally didn't belong to their 'target audience'.

Building Bridges Between the Business and Information/Processes
There are more bridges to build than just those between the 'IT and information management side' and 'the business side'. We've covered this

---

[3] Available from https://www.i-scoop.eu/digital-transformation/digital-transformation-strategy/.

necessity previously from the perspective of information as a bridge builder in the next stage of the information age, whereby information bridges need to exist between back end and front office, content and processes (integration), human and machine and machine to machine (the IoT), raw data and actionable intelligence, and so on. It's equally critical to integrate information/content and processes, with the business and knowledge worker in mind as previously mentioned.

To successfully navigate Digital Transformation and protect against digital disruption, all organizations need to developed three core capabilities says Professor Michael Wade: hyperawareness, informed decision-making and fast execution.

Building Bridges for Actionable Intelligence

Information is ubiquitous and at the centre of Digital Transformation. Data volumes, formats and sources keep growing exponentially. The question for leading companies has become: how do we turn all this data into actionable intelligence in a meaningful, prioritized and profitable way, leading to new opportunities.

At the same time, information management requires a holistic and integrated approach. From digitising and capturing paper-based information to enhancing processes, empowering knowledge workers, better serving customers and getting the right information and intelligence when, where and how they are needed requires several steps and integrations.

Building Human Bridges in a Digital Transformation Strategy

There are ample bridges to be built from a human perspective. Customer-centricity, customer-facing processes and the end-to-end customer experience are key in Digital Transformation strategies. We need more and stronger bridges with customers in ways, which require more depth and breadth (and personalization) than ever.

A Digital Transformation strategy also requires bridges between leaders and 'their people', among others those who are closest to the customers and often feel forgotten and unheard, bridges between various functions and, increasingly, between business execs and leaders from several companies who are building the ecosystems of value which are needed in an economy where new business models and revenue streams de facto increasingly dictate both the business and technology agenda. The customer in the broadest sense (external and internal such as employees, don't forget change management) is the driver behind many bridges to build and instrumental in effectively building them.

Bridges to Build New Ecosystems

The strength of ecosystems and communities of innovation, collaboration and also outsourcing partnerships, defines the strength of the businesses, which are part of them in a culture of co-opetition and co-creation.

Finding new revenue streams together by connecting systems of value and building bridges is key here as well, and is enabled by a technological reality that increasingly revolves around data, actionable intelligence, software and connectivity. This dimension will increase even more with the interconnection of everything and more actionable intelligence opportunities, what the Internet of Things or IoT is really about.

Building Bridges Between Technologies

Another area is the building of bridges between the capabilities of existing and 'emerging' technologies and the potential they offer for the most innovative, which will win in the end.

While many companies already struggle with several of the previously mentioned bridges, this is where the real value can be created in an enterprise-wide and longer term Digital Transformation strategy (Digital Transformation needs a longer term view and strategy). We live in an age where over the past decades new technologies have emerged (some more recently) and gradually became core components of the ways we do business and the ways we live.

Their increasing maturity, as well as their increasing adoption, has led to what called the Nexus of Forces (the convergence of mobile, social, cloud and information has become the platform for digital business. Digital business is the creation of new business designs by blurring the digital and physical worlds). On this site we often refer to the core technologies as the third platform (a term coined by IDC) or SMAC and sometimes SMACIT.

Bridging Technologies and Innovation

When you look at these various technologies, whether it's from their individual traits and evolutions (books are written about each one as they cover many underlying realities and are all de facto umbrella terms) and when you look at how they are often covered, it's easy to forget how they are really part of one single, more holistic, perspective, which is defined by the end goals why we 'invented' them and why we use them.

To do so, you need to grasp what role they play in the bigger picture of Digital Transformation, while identifying the glue that connects them and that in the end enables you to make a solid difference with your strategy. And that's one of the areas where actionable intelligence (what data should become), speed/agility (what the cloud offers), hyper-connectivity and along with it more data (what the IoT, mobility and so on offer), and the intersection of people, purpose, innovation, optimization, information, processes, value and business models come into play.

At the Core of Any Digital Transformation Strategy: Building Bridges with the Future

All the mentioned bridges need to be built. Because here is a reality: some forward-thinking companies have done amazing things using the Industrial Internet of Things and data analysis. They hook up with others with whom they can create new ecosystems of value. Others are doing or will do equally amazing things in other areas.

However, those that in the end will make the difference will not be the technology innovators. It will be individuals and organizations that come up with entirely new ways of innovation and value creation by truly understanding how they can leverage the intelligence that is created in often seemingly unrelated areas by those first movers and, possibly by adding additional capabilities, and who can build bridges between sources and resources in ways we only start understanding today. And to do so, a holistic mind-set, common sense, some distance and a profound understanding of how everything can be connected in the scope of a unique purpose are needed.

Bridging Intent and Achievement: Where Do You Want Your Digital Transformation Strategy to Take You?

Digital Transformation is not a thing, it's partially a journey and partially a goal, but most of all it requires a clear roadmap and strategy with ample room for adjustment in an adaptive way.

The challenge for many executives is to know where they want to head, what they need to get there and how to be sure they successfully did get there with the necessary (intermediate) controls in place.

Digital Transformation Strategy: Planning Mapping and Prioritizing for the Future
We can look at it from two angles:

- On one hand we see that often Digital Transformation is seen as a set of projects, actions and exercises to do or a more enterprise-wide goal to achieve. If you look at it this way, inevitably you need to ask why do I want to transform anything whatsoever, what is that whatsoever and how am I going to get there as mentioned. Essential project management questions and forecasting methods are just a must, even if we tend to forget them and lose ourselves in the technological or organizational questions without the end in mind.
- On the other hand we see that Digital Transformation is often approached as an on-going journey that is more about a continuous business transformation strategy in the scope of technological and societal change. This is obviously a journey that never ends. It's the development of a capacity to act, react and ideally pro-act as societal changes and technological evolutions continue to take place, accelerate and evolve.

Bridging Risk and Certainty
While these questions seem obvious, there are numerous reasons why they are often overlooked and we don't bridge the what, why and how or the intent and achievement.

One of many reasons is that often we are partially and in a sense by definition operating in relatively uncharted territory and aren't sure if we have all the building blocks. That's why it's important to conduct VoC exercises and strategic sessions with various people. It's also why it's important to continue to learn, have a culture of evolution awareness and prioritize. Last but not least, it's why we need a roadmap, as informed as possible, and as mentioned, with the necessary space for failure and balanced risk.

Compare the latter with marketing Return Over Investment (ROI). A good marketer will always strike a balance between activities with more certain outcomes and proven results and activities with less certain or uncertain outcomes which could be unexpectedly high gains or, if it doesn't work that well, losses that don't affect the overall ROI too much.

In exactly the same way and, depending on the scope and breadth/depth of the Digital Transformation strategy, chart the unknowns. What we often see in practice is that the mentioned challenge is not always a matter of uncertainty regarding outcomes but also a matter of uncertainty regarding the "how": the uncertainty regarding what the outcome will look like (as we do speak about change and this something new) is then strengthened by uncertainties whether all the (right) building blocks are foreseen and/or in place to get there.

This uncertainty of missing building blocks or having the wrong ones is often what makes organizations uncertain, as they fear failure in regards with the proper mapping of the needed building blocks (subprojects, people, processes, information sources, change management initiatives, built-in checks and so forth).

What You Can Learn from Leading Incumbents

Many leading 'incumbents' are increasingly setting up environments where they give room to innovation, experimentation and future-oriented sessions, in order to shape their Digital Transformation strategy.

They invite start-ups, newcomers, the often younger generations of technologists who master emerging technologies and/or their existing IT partners (who are also challenged) to showcase, collaboratively think, find talent and potential future scenarios, etc. They set up hackathons, organize brainstorming session days and launch trials in order to prepare for the longer term, as they decreasingly rely upon those first moving 'Digital Transformation experts' who have been repeating the same stories too long too often.

Digital Transformation Strategy and Asking the Right Questions

The main question is: do you build all these bridges and define the goals, set out the strategy and journey, map the required building blocks and barriers, and look at your Digital Transformation strategy and roadmap in a smart way, regardless of all those frameworks out there and, rather, creating the right conditions to get you going?

Here are two things we can already start doing as of right now:

1. Get any 'digital' expertise and culture out of its splendid isolation and let it penetrate the rest of your organization,
2. Look at where the leaks in your business are and where it's clear that you'll need to remove or bridge legacy and necessity, among others in the technologies that are crucial to scale and move faster and better once your strategy is in place.

Some Digital Transformation strategy steps to take into account (and that can be put in the context of the previously mentioned three core capabilities, as well as the, also previously depicted vision, plan, action steps):

- Identify market, evolutions, and pain points.
- Assess/benchmark where you are.
- Analyse/prioritise significant evolutions.
- Map current status with major evolutions and opportunities.
- Assess skillset, culture and readiness.
- Focus on core intangible assets: customers, data.
- Base strategy on where you are and go.
- Include external and internal help.
- Develop a roadmap to get where you need.
- Design for innovation, optimisation, agility and scale.
- Optimize information and data maturity.
- Connect technologies and data (sources) in function of strategy.
- Get clear leadership buy-in.
- Gap bridges with customers and stakeholders.
- Set goals, KPIs and controls.
- Build for ecosystems and platforms.
- Focus on long term with intermediate goals.
- Start where it makes sense (calculated).
- Learn, measure, re-assess, scale, and innovate.

1.3   Measurement

Executing the Change
(Fitzgerald et al. 2013) within Embracing Digital Technology: a New Strategic Imperative, a report developed for *MIT Sloan Management Review* and Capgemini Consulting, affirm that among the obvious obstacles to Digital Transformation is lack of clarity about the pay-off. Companies want to know that they are getting something beneficial from investment in new technologies. Corporate leaders need to leverage metrics to help make Digital Transformation happen.

Making a Case for Digital Transformation
The same authors agree in highlighting that only half of the companies surveyed said they create business cases for their digital initiatives. It can

be hard to gauge a return on investment for emerging technologies. "It is still difficult to compute ROI on many social media activities (at least to the satisfaction of the executive board)" said one survey respondent.

Many organizations struggle to compute ROI. Merely, one-fourth report has established KPIs, in order to measure the impact of companies' Digital Transformation. The three biggest reasons why companies have trouble defining how to successfully define, lack of management skills to carry through on KPIs, and needing cultural changes to make KPIs work.

Those that do measure can be guilty of using fuzzy mathematics. "We are not honest with ourselves about where our capabilities really lie, nor about how we are going to ensure there is accountability for instituting real, competitive change", wrote one survey respondent. "We want to make it seem like we 'get digital' but our Digital Transformation is not holistic, and tends to occur in isolated incidents that are always positioned as 'successful' even when they really aren't".

Digital Transformation is successful when the entire company aligns around a vision, but only a slight majority of companies have given cross-functional committees (37%) or a shared digital units (17%) enterprise-level authority on digital investments. Digirati do much better, at 66%.

Incentives. One obvious way for executives to clear a path for Digital Transformation is to give employees incentives. Bonuses, raise structures, promotions and performance reviews are some of the tools that companies could use, but don't. For beginners, 61% of companies do not tie rewards to Digital Transformation efforts. The companies that do best at Digital Transformation also do the best job of aligning incentives with Digital Transformation efforts: 68% of respondents at Digirati companies do connect Digital Transformation to incentives. Interestingly, these incentives tend to be based on "soft" factors (recognition, personal advancement) rather than "hard" financial factors.

Better incentives might help ease employee concerns about Digital Transformation. One survey respondent noted that "at the operational level, there are some benefits (to Digital Transformation), but much of the day-to-day experience is the feeling of being reduced to being a Victorian machine minder: instead of the software servicing the people, it is the other way around". Another said that the pace of Digital Transformation demanded such speed that it is "at risk of diluting employee morale".

Digital KPIs: Keys to Measuring Digital Transformation Success
(Boulton 2017) defines Digital KPIs as measurable values for evaluating the performance of digital business initiatives. Digital KPIs can help an organization ascertain how far it has progressed on its Digital Strategy and how well it is improving its digital business outcomes.

Gartner's Proctor says that enterprise CIOs seeking to craft digital KPIs should begin by targeting two broad categories.

The first set of KPIs should assess the company's progress in digitizing its current business model by measuring goals in sales, marketing, operations, supply chain, products/services and customer service.

Several restaurants, including TGI Fridays and Wingstop, for example, are using chatbots to help digitize order taking and transactions. Starbucks, Target and several other consumer-facing organizations now let consumers pay for goods from their phones instead of cashiers. CIOs should evaluate such digital operations using metrics that assess adoption rates and business impact relative to traditional operating modes.

A second set of KPIs should assess new revenue sources generated from new digital business models. These KPIs should represent growth, revenue, market share and margin metrics that are differentiated from physical assets.

Proctor & Gamble acquired Dollar Shave Club, giving it a platform from which to sell razors online. Caterpillar acquired Yard Club to rent heavy machines through an online marketplace. Cleveland Clinic sells algorithms for analysing cardiology and oncology through Apervita's online marketplace. These new sources of revenue based on digital models should be evaluated separate from analogue revenue streams to assess how they impact the bottom line.

In the aforementioned context, the following good practices are identified:

While many companies are undertaking Digital Transformations, only about half of CEOs Gartner has surveyed have KPIs to measure digital success, Proctor says. He recommends several steps CIOs can take to measure the value of their digital business:

- <u>Work with senior executives to quantify the extent to which their areas would benefit from digitalization</u>. A CIO might work with a

COO to define how much of the company's manufacturing operations should be digitalized and what benefits to expect.

- Set KPIs and goals that lay out the digital business journey and
  sharpen expected business outcomes. For example, Proctor recommends that healthcare CIOs shift from talking about connected
  healthcare as a vision to proposing the potential percentage of
  patient "visits" that will employ telemedicine. This quantifies a clear
  goal. Then describe the expected benefits of achieving this goal.
- Measure the progress of your digital journey and the business value
  it creates. Here, some KPIs will be "transitional," while others will
  become permanent metrics for business performance as transformation is achieved and digital business becomes standard operating
  procedure. For example, an enterprise that builds a digital ecosystem
  may permanently add ecosystem metrics to its on-going business
  performance KPIs. Good metrics should influence C-suite decisions
  such as budget allocations, business process improvements and culture changes.
- Use KPIs to support specific outcome expectations, such as, "By
  reaching our 2020 goal of digitizing ABC, we will benefit from an X
  increase in these business and financial metrics."
- Don't overdigitize your business. Shoehorning too many customer
  interactions via digital channels can create negative impacts. For
  example, expecting all sales to go through a digital sales channel will
  upset some customers and provide very little chance for high-touch
  engagement. An enterprise should determine the "balance point" at
  which the amount of digitization is ideal for customers and employees. Each KPI should have a balance point that counters the risks
  that come with going all-digital. Silver identifies also three best practices for measuring Digital Transformation KPIs;

In a Gartner survey on Digital Transformation (LeHong 2013), only
about half of the CEOs Gartner surveyed indicated KPIs were in place to
measure digital success.

From (LeHong 2013) experience, this appears to stem from the fact
that digital marketing, experience and information technology executives
have yet to focus on aligning KPIs for Digital Transformation and experience initiatives with the overarching organization or service line goals and
objectives—tying the value of Digital Transformation to the value realized
for the business and clinical enterprise overall.

Ideally, performance measurement and KPIs are built into the Digital Strategy, when the vision and aspirations are first established. This ensures that the Digital Transformation initiatives align with the broader organizational objectives, thus demonstrating not only the progress being made as transformation evolves, but also the ability to link and measure the impact of specific initiatives against the stated organizational goals, such as growth and volume, utilization, access, cost reduction and improved patient and member satisfaction.

Gartner's Proctor suggested digital KPIs should begin by targeting two broad categories:

1. Progress toward digitizing the current business model
2. New revenue sources resulting from new digital business models

While there is no perfect formula for the development of meaningful KPIs, there are some best practices:

1. Assess and quantify the benefits of each digital initiative, working with executive leadership from across the organization to do so. Understand the outcomes they expect to achieve.
2. Establish the KPIs using specific reference to the value each digital initiative is expected to drive. For example, the KPI for Online Patient Scheduling might measure the expected to actual number of online appointments, against the corresponding expected increase in patient volume, or perhaps physician wRVUs, patient member satisfaction or net promoter scores.
3. Make sure to include KPIs that measure the overall progress of the Digital Transformation programme, and establish a scorecard that is visible to the rest of the organization.

Digital Transformation is key strategy for most organizations, and given how competitive the healthcare landscape is these days, the stakes are often high. Following these basic principles and engaging with business executives and clinical leaders will ensure the focus is on the right initiatives and the investments are achieving the desired outcomes.

In accordance with benefits (Boulton 2017), there are no silver bullets or magical formulas for digital business success, but KPIs can help. "The digital KPI is all about understanding where you're making money or improving an existing business model, how to measure that and work with your non-IT execs to achieve new business outcomes that you've set based on the fact that you're going digital," Proctor says. "Outside of that all that you have is a collection of new projects that are using technology to do new stuff and unfortunately that's where most businesses are today."

The stakes are high for CIOs and their C-suite peers to cement a Digital Strategy—and even higher to establish KPIs to measure its effectiveness. Disruption, the kind that Amazon.com has unleashed across the retail landscape, occurs in a market once digital revenue hits 20% of the total. "If you're not [reasonably] digital at that point, you're toast," Proctor says.

Regarding how to manage the KPIs and expectations during Digital Transformation, (Pruitt 2018) Chairman and CEO of Tallwave, considers important to take into account;

Before setting Digital Transformation KPIs, there are a few organizational things you will want to have in place.

Organizational Alignment Comes First

Digital Transformation should set you up for the long-term by giving you a scalable, streamlined approach to business growth. And as such, it starts on the inside, building the internal systems that support even the outward-facing initiatives. With that in mind, having a baseline of what's working and what's not in your organization will provide you a good jumping off point.

Are processes clear, well documented and accessible to everyone? Are all those processes easily repeatable and scalable, and supported by the right technology?

Is there a system in place for hiring the right people, documenting and sharing customer data across different departments, making suggestions for process improvement and acting on it, and getting leadership's approval of major initiatives in an efficient manner? If any of these elements are off, your path to transformation may lead to expensive dead-ends.

Furthermore, does everyone understand the "why" behind the Digital Transformation? There has a to be a deeper purpose driving the transformation and it must serve every initiative, particularly if you are to succeed in getting your team to rally behind it and drive in the same direction. Visibility into the right KPIs will make it clear whether your team is bought in and understands the direction.

Keep in mind, Digital Transformation doesn't happen overnight and building a solid foundation will set your organization up for long-term success. A systems of checks and balances that are frequently analysed will allow you to course correct early on if needed, and it will breath agility into the organization.

Understand Your Organization's Goals

The KPI playbook is different for every organization because goals are different for every organization. KPIs and goals should support and align with the "why" or deeper purpose mentioned above.

That said, there are four basic measurement pillars every organization should consider:

- Improvement of operational efficiency
- Improvement of the internal or external customer experience
- Improvement of your level of agility
- Improvement of business risk management

With those in mind, figure out which align closest with your long-term plans and develop KPIs around them. If you place customer experience at the top of the list, then metrics based on feedback and retention will be most valuable.

Keep Your Expectations Realistic

When you see successful Digital Transformation in your industry, there's a temptation to want to speed up your own process to reach that level of success. Like with any new undertaking of this scale, however, you simply can't expect perfection.

Instead of looking at the finish line, think of KPIs as measurements with a sense of flow. There are plenty of smaller benchmarks within each of your identified KPIs that will help you avoid barriers and roadblocks as much as possible.

Keep in mind, in digitally transforming your company, you're likely pulling several levers at any given time, from up-levelling messaging, to revising your online presence, creating software, implementing automation, building chatbots, etc. Given these realities, <u>some KPIs to consider</u>, could be

- Employee engagement or eNPS (employee Net Promoter Score)
- Customer engagement or NPS (Net Promote Score)
- Usage metrics of web assets (sites) or new digital products/software (mobile apps, web apps, portals, handhelds, etc.)
- Time and cost savings
- Leads
- Revenue
- Growth percentage
- Market share
- Retention rates
- Up times

By setting benchmarks, you'll also be adapting to a key framework of transformation in general—the ability to quickly assess whether a goal is too unrealistic and adjust your process accordingly. If you don't have baselines of your current NPS or customer engagement, for example, setting improvement goals will be little more than a guessing game.

Digital Transformation is an exciting yet oftentimes confounding revolution in business. By knowing what you want to measure and comparing it to where you stand today, you'll lay out a clear as possible map to navigate the many challenges that this new era of technology and innovation poses.

(Overby 2017) outlines the following <u>3 Digital Transformation Metrics</u>; Operational Improvement, Customer Experience and Financial Impact.

Digital Transformation is on every leader's agenda. Yet less than 15% of companies can quantify the impact of their digital initiatives, according to McKinsey's Digital Quotient analysis.

Traditional KPIs are poor indicators of the effectiveness of on-going digital efforts; they are best suited to measuring long-term impact, revealing improvements annually or quarterly. Today's marketplace is changing too rapidly for such horizon gazing, according to Steven Skinner, senior vice president of Cognizant Business Consulting.

As organizations become more agile, the KPIs must be tailored for new operating capabilities," Skinner said in an interview with CMO.com. "Digital Transformation metrics must be aligned with measuring where traction is achieved in a digital capability versus the results achieved at the end of a transformation. This helps assess and refine transformation efforts continuously.

Digital Transformation is a series of changes—the earliest of which are not likely to increase sales or a bump up a Net Promoter Score (Frazier 2018). But incremental change can "lead to more informed and better decision making," said Ashley Stirrup, CMO of software integration provider Talend, in an interview with CMO.com. "Therefore it's very important that companies really think through leading indicators that will help them measure the impact of their digital investments ahead of the actual impact on things like revenue and customer satisfaction".

What's more, according to (Overby 2017), conventional corporate metrics generally offer a narrow view of results, linked to a particular silo in the organization. But Digital Transformation isn't an IT project or a marketing plan, said CarMax CIO Shamim Mohammad, in an interview with CMO.com. "It's a company initiative. The senior leadership needs to be aligned around what they're trying to achieve and, more specifically, they need to organize around business outcomes they can measure every week—in some cases, daily."

Focusing on pre-digital KPIs can be worse than unhelpful—it can thwart transformation. When an organization is not aligned around cross-functional metrics, "each group has a set of objectives that are frequently in conflict with each other, and the business value of the Digital Transformation is left unmeasured", said Michael Witty, director at global technology research and advisory firm ISG.

For digital leaders in the marketing group, that means metrics such as lead generation, campaigns launched, or website visitors fall flat. They "represent a myopic view of the ultimate power and effect of Digital Transformation", said Debbie Qaqish, chief strategy officer at The Pedowitz Group.

What's needed instead are Digital Transformation metrics that span functions and can be measured on a continuous basis to provide the most insight into what's working and what's not. Requisite measures will vary by industry—or even company. But these new metrics designed to track the on-going business impact of Digital Transformation tend to fall in three categories: operational improvement, customer experience, and financial impact.

This author establishes in turn <u>three Digital Transformation Metrics that work for everyone</u>. These metrics are, as detailed below; Operational Improvement, Customer Experience and Financial Aspects

Operational Improvement

Overby also states as a second Digital Transformation metric "Operational improvement", that at its core, Digital Transformation is a continuous improvement initiative as much about changing mind-sets and behaviours as it is bottom-line results. But cultural shifts are difficult to measure. Adoption metrics can be a great proxy, according to Aaron Goldman, CMO of media technology company 4C. "You need to make sure your organization is using the tools you've employed", Goldman said in an interview with CMO.com. "Adoption should be measured no less than weekly. It's the only way to gauge and generate momentum".

One example of continuous improvement is technology stack use and optimization. "Most companies skim the surface in terms of technology use and optimization", Qaqish said. "A key metric of the marketing ops team is to go deep across a fully integrated tech stack that results in improved business performance".

When Cognizant is working on Digital Transformation efforts, "speed to transform" is a key measure, composed of a concise list of metrics that serve as indicators of progress. "We may work with a client to create a new application to reduce process cycle time or reduce rework", Skinner said. "This type of project is successful when processes cycle more quickly or when there are fewer errors—and would appear to be less successful if using only a ROI-style metric".

Other operational or capability metrics that could be useful include task automation, quality metrics, productivity, or application performance, according to ISG's Witty.

Customer Experience

The second Digital Transformation metric established by Overby is the Customer Experience and explains it in the following way.

Most marketing KPIs are "vanity metrics", said Jen Grant, CMO of business intelligence software maker Looker, in an interview with CMO. com. They "feel good but don't really give you a good view of whether your business is healthy or in trouble". Digital transformers will look for signs of improved customer experience.

"You need to be able to measure how successfully a customer can navigate across an ecosystem," said Ingrid Lindberg, president of Kobie Marketing, in an interview with CMO.com. Lindberg became the healthcare industry's first customer experience officer when she took the role at Cigna in 2007. "When leading a Digital Transformation, I look for KPIs that cut across traditional delivery silos and identify measures that can be applied across all of those experiences", she said.

Forget website traffic, bounce rates, and referrals, said Mark Nardone, executive vice president of marketing and new business at PAN Communications, in an interview with CMO.com. He advocated measuring share of voice, customer acquisition costs, and customer lifetime value (CLV), ultimately improving retention rates: "The digital disruption within the industry allows modern marketers to easily measure the value your brand gets from each customer relationship".

CLV tends to get increased attention in Digital Transformation. "It represents the role of marketing across the entire customer lifecycle—not just the top of the funnel", Qaqish said.

Cambell Holt is chief customer officer of Mercer Australia, a $4.2 billion institutional investment, retirement, and health services firm that is investing $50 million over three years on customer-centric Digital Transformation. Measures like NPS and customer satisfaction surveys have their place, Holt told CMO.com. But one of the most important measures for Mercer Australia's Digital Transformation is customer friction. "We measure how much customer effort or time it takes to get something done with us", he said.

Kobie Marketing's Lindberg, who led a Digital Transformation at Prime Therapeutics, said ease of completing tasks is one of the main measures she tracked as well. "But we can't ask channel by channel", she said. "We need to be smart enough to find the spot where we can get the clearest look back possible".

She suggested looking at customer contact in a different way: not by number of calls or average handle times but by types of inquiries. "In health care and finance, I want to see an increase in calls where customers are asking for advice, not trying to solve a problem. In retail, I want to see an increase in calls of customers asking for more information or for a deeper connection to a product or service, not complaints", she said.

"When you begin a Digital Transformation, you should see simple tasks being diverted, which means that your more intricate will affect your average handle time".

Financial Impact

Finally, in relation to Financial Impact as the third Digital Transformation metric, CMOs and other Digital Transformation leaders are being held to significant growth targets. But the impact on revenue or margins does not happen overnight. Digital leaders should instead seek out measures that are meaningful when monitored on a daily or weekly basis and give a good indication whether efforts are headed in the right direction.

Since taking over as CMO of Bynder three years ago, Lidia Lüttin has focused empowering more data-driven decision-making at the brand management software company. "It can be difficult at times, as in this case Digital Transformation does not only involve 'being digital' but changing the mind-set of people", Lüttin tol CMO.com. "And change management can be a strenuous process".

She illustrated the financial value of those sometimes, painful efforts by tracking increases in productivity or revenue per employee and decreases in customer acquisition costs. "By freeing up brainpower, we get more new initiatives as we bring down the number of repetitive tasks, which is more efficient for our bottom line, while simultaneously being a more attractive and innovative place to work for our talent", she said.

For David Gee, CMO of Zuora, whose SaaS business is built around enterprise software subscribers, the magic financial metrics are annual recurring revenue, recurring profit margin, and growth efficiency. "Tracking growth efficiency, or how much it costs to acquire $1 annual contract value, gives companies a sense if they effectively transforming", he said in an interview with CMO.com.

It's critical to look for financial measures that provide incentives for the entire enterprise to embrace on going digital change, ISG's Witty said. For example, one retailer is measuring gross margin by category, rather than by channel, to track how well the organization is working together to drive sales. That financial data complements operational metrics for channel integration and customer-focused KPIs measuring share of wallet, loyalty, customer growth, and cross-channel satisfaction.

References

Boulton, C. (2017). *Digital KPIs: Your Keys to Measuring Digital Transformation Success.* Retrieved March 19, 2018, from https://www.cio.com/article/3236446/digital-transformation/digital-kpis-your-keys-to-measuring-digital-transformation-success.html and https://www.cio.com/article/3211428/digital-transformation/what-is-digitaltransformation-a-necessary-disruption.html.

Fitzgerald, M., Kruschwitz, N., Bonnet, D., & Welch, M. (2013). Embracing Digital Technology: A New Strategic Imperative. *MIT Sloan Management Review* and Capgemini Consulting. Retrieved October 2, 2018, from https://sloanreview.mit.edu/projects/embracing-digital-technology/.

Frazier, S. (2018). *4 Change Management Best Practices for Net Promoter® and CX Programs.* Retrieved October 2018, from https://customergauge.com/blog/4-change-management-best-practices-for-net-promoter-and-cx-programs.

LeHong, H. (2013). *Digital Business KPIs: Defining and Measuring Success.* Retrieved October 4, 2016, from https://www.gartner.com/doc/3237920/digital-business-kpis-defining-measuring.

Matt, C., Hess, T., & Benlian, A. (2015). Digital Transformation strategies. *Business & Information Systems Engineering, 57*(5), 339–343. Retrieved March 2016, from http://dx.doi.org.ezp-02.lirn.net/10.1007/s12599-015-0401-5.

Overby, S. (2017). *3 Digital Transformation Metrics That Work For Everyone.* CMO.com. Retrieved November 10, 2017, from https://www.cmo.com/features/articles/2017/9/12/3-digital-transformation-metrics-that-work-for-everyone.html#gs.5A8ExWM.

Pruitt, J. (2018). *How to Manage Your KPIs and Expectations During Digital Transformation. Are You Looking at the Right Data to Match Your Company Goals? It Will Make All the Difference.* Retrieved October 2, 2018, from https://www.inc.com/jeff-pruitt/3-things-to-know-when-setting-digital-transformation-kpis.html.

Solis, B. (2013). *The Six Stages of Digital Transformation Maturity.* Retrieved August 28, 2018, from https://www.cognizant.com/whitepapers/the-six-stages-of-digital-transformation-maturity.pdf.

CHAPTER 5

Digital Transformation Strategy Framework

This chapter presents the results of the research work carried out.

This book presents as it main contribution the construction of a strategic Digital Transformation operational framework, necessary and adaptable to any type of company and sector of activity. Therefore, the strategic framework suggested includes the patterns, actions, approaches and several measures that are detailed below.

- A pattern for preparing Internal Training Plan adapted to Digital Strategy.
- A Tool for diagnosing the level of digital maturity and a Scorecard tool for the assessment and actions associated with the scope of the optimum degree of digital maturity).
- A Digital Transformation Strategic Framework (elements and phases).
- A Digital Transformation Strategy Plan (phases and actions).
- A Digital Transformation Strategy's Balance Scorecard.

1 THE RELEVANCE OF BUSINESS MODELS AND THE EXISTENCE OF A DIGITAL STRATEGY

In this new age of knowledge and digital economy, business models are assuming increasing importance as elements of strategic innovation and main driving forces to firm's competitiveness. Those circumstances are creating new demands to understand how firms design and systematize their

A. Landeta Echeberria, *A Digital Framework for Industry 4.0*, https://doi.org/10.1007/978-3-030-60049-5_5

operations, generate value for costumers and draw the costs structure, revenues and profits to be distributed, all elements of a business model (Chesbrough and Rosenbloom 2002). But also as firms address the characterization and measurement of innovation practices (Adams et al. 2006) and endorses the complexity of business modes in relation to strategy and the management of innovation emerging from IT (Powell 1992).

Managing digital innovation become an important issue not only for contemporary firms, by nature more open for innovation, but for all firms, namely those living a Digital Transformation process (Holmstro and Nyle 2015).

Bharadwaj et al. (2013), underlining the rapid growth of a digital world during the last decade, assumed the existence of a digital business strategy which is inherently simultaneously strategic and technological due to the ubiquitous presence of digital in all dimensions of decision, overlapping business strategy with IT strategy.

They have defined digital business strategy has an "organizational strategy formulated and executed by leveraging digital resources to create differential value" (Bharadwaj et al. 2013, p. 472).

Harmancioglu et al. (2009) introduced the concept of resource fit, which refers to strategic fit resources for a new initiative. Based on this perspective, Digital Transformation begins with the evaluation of resources so as to generate a firm's competitive advantage and the identification of sources of synergy or fit. Apparently, resource fit provides a broadened view that considers both resource-based theory and strategic fit view to extend our understanding of Digital Transformation. However, to date, little research has exploited the concept of resource fit in Digital Transformation; thus, the critical factors for making a successful Digital Transformation are still largely unexplored.

2   Construct of Strategic Framework

This strategic framework is composed of a research model, elements, phases of development, actions and activities, which will be described below.

2.1   *Research Model and Methodology*

Research Model
Due to the nature of this research, a methodological approach based on a combination of synthetic and analytical methods was chosen with a view

to develop a Digital Tranformation Research Strategy Model for companies within the Industry 4.0 framework.

Said combination will facilitate greater understanding of the phenomenon and its subsequent application. This focus adjusts to the research as it is intended to investigate how to prepare a digital transformation strategy framework within the context of Industry 4.0. The confirmation of a digital strategy in the context of companies with the aim of digitizing existing business models and/or implementing improvements to the existing one is a relatively recent phenomenon that continues to develop within different industrial sectors.

In this sense, the study primarily uses this methodological combination in which, data, trends and policy initiatives collected will be used as a source from which conclusions can be drawn that may drive the development of a specific strategic focus.

The synthetic method is a reasoning process that tends towards rebuilding the whole based on the elements distinguished by the analysis. In short, it consists of a methodical and brief explosion. In other words, we must say that synthesis is a mental process aimed at obtaining a thorough understanding of the essence of know-how in all its parts and particularities. Synthesis means reconstructing and re-integrating the parts of the whole. However, this operation implies overcoming the analytical procedure, as not only does it represent the mechanical reconstruction of the whole, as this will not allow for the advancement of knowledge but that it implies the understanding of the essence of same, to ascertain the basic aspects and relations from the perspective of the totality. There is no synthesis without analysis, as (Engel 1999) said, as analysis provides the raw material with which synthesis can be performed.

The analytic-synthetic model is a route to knowledge as involves analysis (from the Greek *análisi*, meaning 'decomposition') that is, the separation of a tone in its parts and constitutive elements. It is supported, therefore, on the belief that in order to know a phenomenon it is necessary to break it down into its parts. In contrast with that manifested, the synthetic method involves synthesis (from the Greek *synthesis*, meaning 'union'), that is to say, the union of elements to form a whole.

Thus, the resolution method with heuristic content since in Descartes's own formulation (Descartes 1983), in his "Regulae ad directionem ingenii and in his Geometric" (Descartes 1983), the method can be formally presented, broken down into a series of steps, which the resolver literally goes through: (1) A heuristic reading of the problem statement that reduces it to a list of quantities and relationships between quantities, (2) Choice of a quantity to be represented with a letter (or of a few quantities that are going to be represented with different letters). (3) Representation of other quantities by algebraic expressions that describe the relationship (arithmetic) that these quantities have with others that have been previously represented by an algebraic letter or expression. (4) Establishment of an equation (or so many different letters that have been decided to introduce in the second phase), matching two expressions, of those described in the third step, that represent the same amount. (5) Transformation of the equation in a canonical way. (6) Application of the solution formula or algorithm to the equation in a canonical way. (7) Interpretation of the result of the equation in terms of the problem.

The analytical judgement involves the decomposition of the phenomenon into its constitutive parts. It is a mental process that divides the complete representation of a phenomenon into its parts.

The synthetic judgement, on the contrary, consists of systematically joining the heterogeneous elements of a phenomenon with the purpose of rediscovering the individuality of everything observed. Synthesis means the act of unifying the disparate parts of a phenomenon. However, synthesis is not the sum of the partial contents of a reality: synthesis adds to the parts of the phenomenon something that can only be acquired on the whole, in its singularity.

Consequently, and taking the methodological focus mentioned previously and the nature of this work into account, the construction of the analytic-synthetic model combines the assembly of a tool to measure the level of maturity with an evolution in accordance with the diagnosis from a strategic perspective driven towards the preparation of a development plan for the digital transformation of companies.

Methodology
The design of the analytical and systematic research methods of this work is illustrated in Fig. 5.1.

Due to the nature of this research, a methodological focus based on new, exploratory research was chosen. This research also intends to provide a general and approximate view in order to develop an Internal Training Plan model adapted to the digital strategy of the company within the framework of Industry 4.0.

As a barely explored, emerging area and, furthermore, one where the nature of the subject of study does not allow for the formulation of a precise hypothesis, Industry 4.0, understood as the fourth industrial

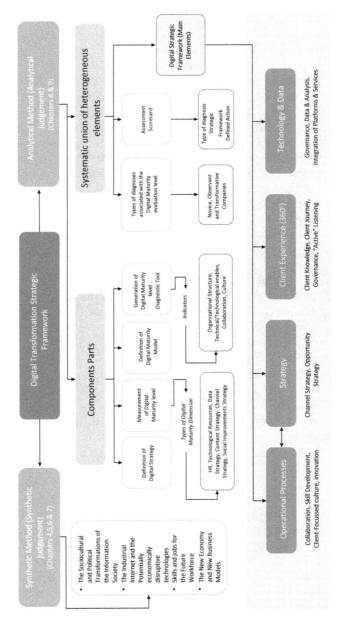

Fig. 5.1 Research model and methodology. (Source: Author's own)

revolution, is a new phenomenon that is so new that it does not allow a systematic description at present. So, resources for researchers are still insufficient to undertake more in-depth work.

Fitness of Research Method Used in a DT Strategy Model for Businesses

The objective of the DT strategy is to create the capacity necessary for taking maximum advantage of the possibilities and opportunities offered by new technologies and their impact in a more rapid, better and more innovative way in the future. A DT journey needs a phase-based focus with a clear roadmap that involves a variety of interested parties, beyond the silos and limitations, internal and external. This DT Strategy Framework takes into account the fact the final objectives will continue to advance given that digital technology is a continuous journey, just like digital change and innovation are.

Therefore, the DT Strategy is the process of identifying, articulating and executing digital opportunities that extend the competitive advantage of the organisation.

So, if the DT Strategy is a process, it cannot be forgotten that a process represents progress, from an initial starting point, to the approaching and surpassing landmarks, both identified and unknown as well as with measurement. Therefore, the proposed solution goes through the application of the metric presented below.

In order to build up a *research method used in a DT strategy model for businesses*, as a starting point the doctoral thesis "A Digital Transformation Strategy Model for companies within the Industry 4.0 framework" by the same author as the current study was taken.

Therefore, the synthetic model research, contains a review of the scientific literature mentioned above, mainly topics related to sociocultural and political transformations of the Information Society, the Industrial Internet and the potentially economically disruptive technologies, skills and the jobs of the future and the New Economy and new business models.

Secondly, the parts components of the strategic framework were defined; definition of DT, measuring of digital maturity model, generation of digital maturity evaluation level tool, associating them with processes inherent in the construction of a plan of digital transformation of a part.

Third, following the guidelines of the Analytical Method (systematic union of heterogeneous elements; specifically, types of diagnoses associated with the digital maturity evaluation level and assessment scorecard) we have resulted in the main elements of the DT Strategic Framework; Strategy, Technology & Data, Client Experience (360°) and Operational Processes.

The New Economy, New Business Models & Digital transformation of the business landscape

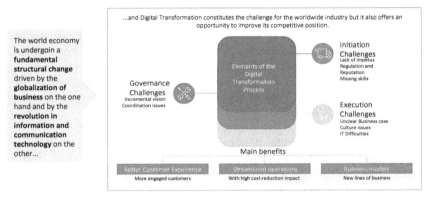

Fig. 5.2 Strategy model research methodology; the DT strategy framework (interrelation of elements, actions, activities, phases and tools). (Source: Author's own elaboration from Digital Transformation: A roadmap for billion-dollar organizations study (2011))

The elements, phases of development, actions and tools related to the DT Strategy Framework will include those presented graphically in Fig. 5.2.

Phases of Development
The Phases and Actions/Activities interrelation of the DT Strategy Framework will result in the creation of a Strategic DT Operational Framework complementary to the DT Strategic Framework.
The aforementioned phases are detailed below.

- Phase 1. Insights and Analysis: understanding the needs and priorities of the people who are at the core of your digital revolution including your customers, stakeholders, employees and executives. Analyse internal performance and sales data to understand where the biggest value is External Digital Analysis, Customer Experience Mapping and Digital Value Chain Analysis.
- Phase 2. Digital Framework: creating a framework that allows the company to addresses digital goals and objectives; The Iteration Model, Big Idea/Mission/Vision, Digital Objectives and UVP.
- Phase 3. The Digital Scope: addressing the company's approach to key areas of Digital and outlining the purpose, objectives and key

initiatives and challenges of each channel; Website(s), Online Content, Digital Advertising/SEM/SEO, CRM, Social, Mobile and ERP.

- Phase 4. Execution & Governance: prioritizing the plan, taking into account, which needs are the most urgent and important as well as current resources, timelines and budgets. Digital business models become more agile we're forced to create plans that are iterative. Unlike traditional business planning, looking 3–5 years ahead is rarely realistic and accurate budgeting can be nearly impossible; Project priorities, Project team(s) and Accountability and Progress Reporting / KPI's.

And, the interrelations between Phases, Tools, Patterns, Actions, Approaches and Measures derive in solutions understood as tools of different utility during the development of the phases mentioned above, as can be seen in Fig. 5.3.

3   Tools

Therefore, in parallel to the DT Strategic Framework, this research work presents as one of the contributions, the construction of a Strategic DT operational framework, necessary and adaptable to any type of company and sector of activity.

Moreover, the DT Strategic Framework is a compendium of tools build ad hoc that will allow the development of the actions inherent to the conformation of the Business DT Plan.

Furthermore, carried out together with the DT Strategy Framework, both frameworks will ensure a Business DT Plan design and execution with grants from an operational and strategic perspective, respectively (Fig. 5.4).

Consequently, the strategic framework suggested includes the patterns, actions, approaches and several measures that are detailed below and fully explained in "A Digital Transformation Strategy Model for companies within the Industry 4.0 framework"—this study author´s PhD thesis—(useful documentation for companies not interested in knowing the results of this work from a purely academic perspective).

- Model for preparing Internal Training Plan adapted to DT Strategy.
- Tool for diagnosing the level of digital maturity and a Scorecard tool for the assessment and actions associated with the scope of the optimum degree of digital maturity).

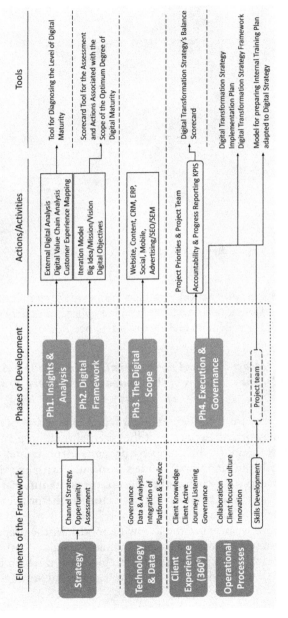

Fig. 5.3 Digital transformation strategy framework (phases and actions/activities interrelation). (Source: Author's own)

Strategic Digital Transformation Operational Framework
(Tools, Patterns, Action, Approaches and Measures)

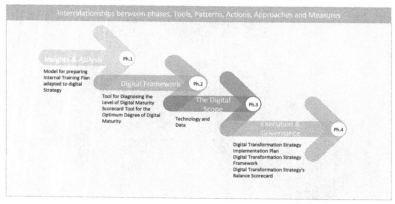

Fig. 5.4 Strategic digital transformation operational framework. (Source: Author's own)

- Digital Transformation Strategic Framework (elements and phases).
- Digital Transformation Strategy Plan (phases and actions).
- Digital Transformation Strategy´s Balance Scorecard.

3.1 Model Proposed for Internal Training Plan Adapted to the Digital Strategy of the Company Within the Framework of Industry 4.0

Taking into account the inherent and integrated function of the new competence framework, the concept of the internal training plan aligned with the Digital Strategy of the company presents a substantial change comparatively with the traditional models associated with the design of said plans. The main change lies in the conception of the internal training plan as a driving force and complementary factor for the principal axes of the Digital Strategy of the company.

Thus, below, we propose the following model for the preparation of the internal training plan adapted to the company's Digital Strategy, including the basic model, integration of the strategic lines to which the plan contributes and general indicators relayed to the Digital Strategy (Table 5.1).

Table 5.1 Model for preparing internal training plan adapted to Digital Strategy

Institutions / Administration:	
Justification of the specific plan:	
Objectives of the specific training plan	
Strategic axes they contribute to	Leadership
	Clients
	Organisational culture
	People
	Technology
Phases of the assessment they contribute to:	F1.- Analyse the expert environment
	F2.- Definition of business model
	F3.- Define target market
	F4.- Review and optimise
	F5.- Improve client experience
	F6.- Foster a new organisational culture
	F7.- Adopt the most appropriate technological solutions
	F8.- Discover the new business ecosystems
	F9.- Develop scorecards based on analysis for the Digital Strategy
Areas of electronic competence to be associated	Plan, Build, Run, Enable, Manage.

(*continued*)

Table 5.1 (continued)

General indicators relating to the Digital Transformation strategy	Leadership (organisational structure)	Technology
	Our company has allocated structural resources for the development of ICTs.	ICT tolos are part of the daily comercial processes of the company.
	The management have clearly defined how to integrate ICTs in the processes of our company (vision/strategy).	Our company uses a broad range of technological tools.
	The roles and responsibilities (with respect to the management of information) are clearly defined within the organisation.	Employees adapt the way they process information so that others can understand it and reuse it.
	Our company is conducting an active transition of the company's physical processes to digital.	**Organisational culture**
		There is full support between employees for the exchange of digital information.
	Human capital (training)	Employees are conscious of the aggregate value of the exchange of digital information (for example, through an ambassador).
	The company is investing in the necessary skills and training actions. It is recognised that the effective use of ICTs requires continuous learning.	Our company possess the necessary skills to exchange digital information effectively.
	The roles and responsibilities (with respect to the management of information) are clearly defined within the organisation.	The exchange of digital information is integrated in the way we work.
		Client
		The company uses information to anticipate the needs of the client.
Measures of the specific training plan		The company compiles data from external sources and applies predictive analysis techniques.
		The company listens to clients and offers feedback, both to favourable comments and complaints and criticism.
		The company understands how clients interact and pays attention to the changes that announce trends.
		The company involves the client, making them a participant, making them an active part of the business through the different channels and offers, with the aim of cementing their loyalty.
Definition of the measure		
Evaluation and monitoring		
Specific indicators of the measure		**Specific indicator of the measure**
Expected value:		**Expected value:**
Final value:		**Final value:**
Qualitative value of the measure		
Suggestions for improvement		
Qualitative assess-ment of the plan	Suggestions for improvement	General associated evaluations

Source: Author's own based on the Lifelong Learning Strategic Plan prepared by the Directorate General for Professional Training. *Sub-directorate General for Lifelong Learning, Spanish Ministry of Education, Culture and Sport.* European Commission

Table 5.2 Integration of new mechanisms in instructional design associated with the programmes inherent in the internal training plan adapted to the Digital Strategy

General context: Internal Training Plan adapted to Digital Strategy
Specific context *(aimed at business units and/or departments)*
General objectives of proposed training actions *(may be those that appear in the Strategic Plan of the Department/Organisation)*
Strategic-digital objectives *(will obey those established in the Internal Training Plan adapted to the Digital Strategy)*
Training actions proposed: description inherent in each training action; *the designation of the action, the area or ambit of knowledge, the organic centre or administrative unit of the Department; the criteria for prioritising training actions; the criteria for selection of participating personnel; the didactic format (preferably e-learning); the duration in hours of the training activity; the calendar of execution foreseen and the form of assessment of training activities.*
Polarising criteria of the shares
The training activities must be prioritised to respond to the urgency of needs estimated by each Department and/or Business Unit but aligned with the objectives and guidelines proposed in the Internal Training Plan adapted to the Digital Strategy.

Priority	Area of Knowledge (Competence Dimension)	Activity	Organic centre (Department/ Business Unit)	Student Profile	Selection criteria	Evaluation

Source: Author's own based on a standard departmental training plan model

The model proposed must also contain a series of training programmes attached to the internal training plan (*see the proposed training actions in Sect. 3.3. Technological Evolution and Training-Business Strategy*)—with elements and characteristics such as those described below, at organic, structural and competence level (Table 5.2):

3.2 Tool for Diagnosing the Level of Digital Maturity

This tool allows for the assessment of the maturity of the company's ICTs with respect to the exchange of digital information. The questionnaire to be completed on the part of the interested company allows it to assess its digital maturity based on four indicators:

- Organisational structure;
- Technical-technological enablers;
- Collaboration; and
- Culture.

The assessment consists of 30 questions on these four elements relating to the maturity of ICTs. It should be possible to complete it in around five minutes. Once the assessment is carried out, the tool generates different types of diagnoses that allow for better use of the ICTs, for the positioning of the organisation in the market to thrive and to set the basis for the construction and/or updating of the company's Digital Transformation plan.

This assessment model is based on Building Information Modelling (BIM), a process that involves the use of communication protocols, data directories, ICT tools and existing standards within the European e-learning macro.

The questionnaire is based on the maturity models described by the Construction Industry Council in PAS1192-2 and by (Succar 2009) in his article "Building information Modelling framework: A research and delivery foundation for industry stakeholders[1]".

On choosing the response that best adapts to the company's situation, notions are obtained regarding how to improve the maturity of ICTs. The responses such as "Totally disagree", "I disagree", "partially agree", etc. are treated confidentially and are not stored. After completing the questionnaire, the areas of improvements are shown and the information useful when it comes to taking the digital maturity of the company to the next level is presented (Table 5.3).

- The ranges to obtain the diagnosis areA larger number of "Totally disagree" and "I disagree" responses is typical of a novice company.
- A large number of "Partly agree" and "I agree" responses obtained is typical of an observant company.
- A large number of "Totally disagree" and "I disagree" responses obtained is typical of a transformative company.

The tool is comprised of two main parts: the front end (the part of the tool visible to users, in which they can see and respond to questions) and the back end (the part where the questions are created, the tools are configured, questions are added and responses are analysed).

---

[1] Questionnaire available from https://www.academia.edu/170356/Building_Information_Modelling_framework_a_research_and_delivery_foundation_for_industry_stakeholders.

Table 5.3   List of questions raised in the questionnaire

Organisational structure

01. Our company has allocated structural resources for the development of ICTs.
02. The management have clearly defined how to integrate ICTs in the processes of our companies (vision/strategy).
03. It is recognised that the effective use of ICTs requires continuous learning.
04. Our company is investing in the necessary skills.
05. The roles and responsibilities (with respect to the management of information) are clearly defined within the organisation.
06. Before cooperating, clear (contractual) agreements are established with our company partners on communication procedures.

Technical-technological enablers

07. ICT tools are part of our daily commercial processes.
08. All information is stored digitally using *software* tools and is accessible and editable by others.
09. Our company uses a broad range of technological tools.
10. It is possible to directly exchange information between our information systems without interference.
11. Our processes are designed on the basis of open standards.

Collaboration

12. Our company knows the tools and standards of ICTs that our company partners use.
13. Our digital information is stored/described in accordance with a standardised dictionary of data.
14. Our communication procedures are defined in accordance with open communication standards (protocols).
15. The (technical) information stored in the different working procedures is reused for multiple purposes (collaborative work).
16. Different actors, both internal and external, work simultaneously on a model and information is exchanged in all phases of the life cycle of the project (for example, design, construction, operation phases).

Culture

17. There is full support between employees for the exchange of digital information.
18. Employees are conscious of the aggregate value of the exchange of digital information (for example, through an ambassador).
19. Our company possess the necessary skills to exchange digital information effectively.
20. The exchange of digital information is integrated in the way we work.
21. Our company is conducting an active transition of the company's physical processes of to digital.
22. Employees adapt the way they process information so that others can understand it and reuse it.

Clients

23. The company uses information to anticipate the needs of the client.
24. The company compiles data from external sources and applies predictive analysis techniques.

(*continued*)

Table 5.3 (continued)

25. The company groups internal data such as: activity of client on company website, loyalty programmes and social media.
26. The company listens to clients and offers feedback, both to favourable comments and complaints and criticism.
27. The company understands how clients interact and pays attention to the changes that announce trends.
28. The company is capable of identifying its strong points (aspects reflected in increased customer satisfaction).
29. The company personalises, multiplying customisation and increasing the possibilities of the client feelings important, valued and unique for that reason.
30. The company involves the client, making them a participant, making them an active part of the business through the different channels and offers, with the aim of cementing their loyalty.

Would you like to consult the diagnosis at some point in the future? Please leave your email address below and the results of the assessment will be sent to you.

Source: Author's own (adapted for the connection between this diagnosis and the construction of the company development plan from the Connect and Construct project 2014, finance by the European Commission. Available at: http://www.connectandconstruct.eu/microsite/digital_maturity.php

Interpreting the Diagnosis Results

Types of Diagnoses Associated with the Level of Digital Maturity of the Company

Diagnosis of the Digital Maturity Results of the "Novice Company" Principal Characteristics[2]

As a novice, it is in the early stages of the exchange of digital information. It is communicating with clients and commercial partners but not in the most coordinated and efficient way possible. It is not familiar with the ICT tools currently available and has difficulty ascertaining the aggregate value of tools. The ICTs used in the organisation support the conventional processes, but are not configured in a manner that completely facilitates innovation in their daily commercial processes. Within the company there are limited financial resources available to develop ICT solutions and the current systems lack interoperability. The development of an ICT vision or strategy has begun. However, it is possible that employees, clients and the administration are not

[2] The principal characteristics are merely a general profile. The real profile may and will be different.

Strategic Digital Transformation Operational Framework

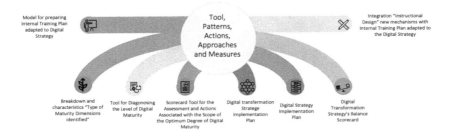

Fig. 5.5 "Novice Company" results. (Source: Author's own (adaptation) for the connection of the current diagnosis with the construction of the company's development plan From the Connect and Construct (2014))

aware of the benefits of ICTs and that the exchange of digital information is not compatible with the rest of the company (Fig. 5.5).

Graphic Representation of the Diagnosis

The Road to Follow (Recommendations)
As a novice company, it must consider investing in obtaining the correct growth in ICTs. The company has the opportunity to progress very much in taking its first toward a digital future. To obtain knowledge, it will discover the benefits of exchanging digital information. This is a trivial step to win the full support of the company. Where the administration knows the benefits, the next step would be to take advantage of this knowledge for an entire organisation. In terms of use of ICTs, the company must attempt to discover what ICT tools are available currently and which might help the digital exchange of information. In the end investing in ICT solutions and having a clear vision can help and streamline the effective development of daily processes. It is crucial to generate an organisational culture based on the use of ICTs.

Diagnosis of Digital Maturity: Results for "Observant Company"
Principal Characteristics
As an observant company, starts recognising the benefits of the exchange of digital information. Have clear ideas about how the exchange of digital information can contribute to the organisation. Is familiar with ICT tools

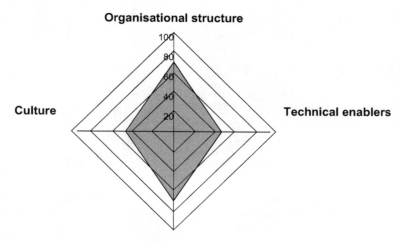

Fig. 5.6 "Observant Company" results. (Source: Author's own (adaptation for the connection of the current diagnosis with the preparation of the development plan of the company starting with the (Connect and Construct 2014))

currently available. Is (digitally) communicating with clients and commercial partners but not in the most coordinated and efficient way possible. The exchange of digital information is gaining support in the organisation is ready to make the change but may be confronted with limited resources. Also, the organisation may not be structured in a way that completely facilitates the exchange of digital information. That is to say, it may not be clear who is responsible for ICTs and how to develop the strategy or vision. What's more, it may also be faced with resistance within middle management (Fig. 5.6).

Graphic Representation of the Diagnosis

The Road to Follow (Recommendations)
As an observant company, is already, to a great extent, storing digital information and using ICT tools. The next step is to begin collaborating digitally with commercial partners in a coordinated and efficient way. That is, it must consider investing in a central storage solution (e.g. document management system, models server, etc.) for all documents and models.

This will allow for the exchange of documents simultaneously with all commercial partners and ensure that all are working with the correct and most recent versions.

Begins to adapt to the hyper-connectivity of the client and to forecast new trends from the information available on the network.

Moreover, it must begin to realise standards partners' use and how the information flow can be improved. Also beginning to become familiar with the use of open standards: these allow for collaboration with others in a softer, more efficient way.

The firm has clear ideas about how the exchange of digital information can contribute to the organisation. The next step might be to formalise these ideas by coming up with a clear strategy and vision on the development of ICTs. It must also consider assigning fixed roles and responsibilities for ensuring these objectives are met.

Employees, clients and middle management may be reluctant to embrace these changes Train employees in the use of ICTs to help them soften the transition, make sure employees are more experienced and active with ICTs.

Diagnosis of the Digital Maturity of the Results
of the "Transformative Company"
Principal Characteristics
As a transformative company, it belongs to the most developed organisation in terms of the exchange of digital information; it lives and breathes ICTs and digital collaboration. It sees its projects as an integrated process over the course of the life cycle. All the information is used an exchanged in open standards. It uses a standardised common vocabulary (e.g. data dictionaries) and uses communication protocols when collaborating. These are mentioned contracts with commercial partners. The company is expert in knowledge of ICT tools and standards. Moreover, all members of the organisation are aware of the benefits of the exchange of digital information and have the experience and training necessary to use in efficiently and effectively. The exchange of digital information is integrated in the way we work. It is part of the way of doing business and stimulating others to do the same. A clear strategy and vision is captures and the roles and responsibilities for the development of the ICTs are defined (Fig. 5.7).

Organisational structure

Fig. 5.7   "Transformative Company" results. (Source: Author's own (adaptation for the connection with the construction of the evolution plan of the company from the Connect and Construct project, finance by the European Commission)

Graphic Representation of the Diagnosis

The Road to Follow (Recommendations)
As transformative, the company is very mature in terms of the exchange of digital information. In particular, in relation to ICT, without giving up the pursuit of continued improvement. Therefore, the company must continually focus on developing its skills and see the exchange of digital information as a continuous learning experience.

Moreover, it must attempt to be a model to follow for its partners and other organisations. To propagate the exchange of digital information in an attempt to ensure other organisations become aware of the need. During the digital future, which will be more beneficial for all and motivated to work in a standardised way, that everyone can understand and apply.

Takes advantage of the information to anticipate the needs of the client. Through the hyperconnectivity provided by the information on the network, foresees new technologies, offers products and services adjusted to the tastes and preferences of each customer, anticipates the demand for a specific product to be able to adjust production, optimising the production and logistics procedures and, definitively, the management of the *stocks*.

3.3   *Scorecard and Actions Associated with Reaching Digital Maturity*

Scorecard Tool for the Assessment and Actions Associated with the Scope of the Optimum Degree of Digital Maturity

As pointed out above, the tool for the assessment of the level of digital maturity of the company in the framework of Industry 4.0 is conceived as a tool to evaluate the starting point of an organisation based on four key dimensions that have been demonstrated.

Based on the results-diagnostics obtained, having completed the assessment questionnaire proposed in Sect. 3.2 of this work the *scorecard* for the digital maturity of the company allows for a series of actions-recommendations relating to the objective of optimum level of digital maturity to be obtained. This second tool is fundamental to the definition of the Digital Strategy, inherent in the preparation of a development plan for the Digital Transformation of the company.

And so, the *scorecard* will adapt to the client's results, the qualitative responses given in the questionnaire and the knowledge of the industry in question.

One aspect worth highlighting when it comes to leading clearly defined digital business strategies are that strategy should completely integrate with the corporate strategy.

Below we will show how the company can use the scorecard based on the score obtained in the tool's diagnostic questionnaire to promote the Digital Strategy (Table 5.4):

1. Catalyst to create discussions between the management team on digital strengths and weaknesses
2. Dashboard for planning associated with the digital and technological roadmap of the entire organisation
3. Rallying of the organisation around a common vision
4. Identifying the high- and medium-impact projects

Table 5.4 Scorecard and actions associated with reaching digital maturity

Type of diagnosis knowledge of the industry 4.0	"Novice Company" Results (Basic level ICT) Actions	"Observant Company" (Medium level ICT) Actions	"Transformative Company" (High level ICT) Actions
Strategy Governance Channel Strategy Assessment of opportunity	(1) Invest in obtaining the correct knowledge with respect to the ICTs (2) Obtain knowledge of the benefits of exchanging digital information.	(1) Consider and assign clear roles and responsibilities for ensuring these objectives are met. (2) Prepare the reaction inherent in the rejection associated with the management of the change (employees and middle management be reluctant to embrace these changes). (3) Know what standards partners use and how information flows can be improved. (4) Familiarise oneself with the use of open standards. (5) Formalise these ideas formulating a clear strategy and vision on the development of ICTs.	Moreover, it must attempt to be a model to follow for its partners and other organisations.

Client experience (client 360) Client knowledge Client journey Governance "Active" listening	(1) Discover what ICT tools are available currently and which can help the digital exchange of information. (2) Create a holistic vision of the clients based on the appropriate choice of adequate technology. (3) Takes advantage of the information to anticipate the needs of the client. (4) Manage to anticipate the needs of the client offer products and services adjusted to the tastes and preferences of each customer and, in the case of customers as a group, foresee the demand for a specific product to be able to adjust production, optimising the production and logistics process and, ultimately, the management of *stocks*). (5) Use the collection of data through mechanisms capable of collating information on purchases made by a customer (loyalty card, user accounts, etc.) and the information generated based on the transactional data of companies. (6) Anticipate demand and new trends from the information available on the network (*benchmarking*).	Meta; Client 360, inherent actions: (1) Define a client identity (2) Group internal data (transaction information, collected client service data and client satisfaction questionnaires or studies, client activity on company websites, loyalty programmes and social media). (3) Compile data from external sources (trends and events, lifestyle, geographic and demographic profiles, habits and data that allow for a competitor analysis to be carried out). (4) Apply predictive analysis techniques: combining all the information contained, analytical techniques can be applied *cross selling* and *up selling* or the possibilities of lead conversion.	The organisation has gained from the integration of information, in terms of knowledge and vision, but there are still 5 steps left to take: (1) Listen to the client and offer feedback. (2) Understand how clients interact. (3) Identify our strong points as a brand. (4) Personalise. Multiply customisation and increase the possibilities of the client feeling important and feeling valued by the company and unique. (5) Listen to the client. Make them participate, becoming an active part of the business through the different channels and offers, with the aim of cementing their loyalty.
Technology and data Governance Data and trends Platform integration Partner integration	(1) Investing in ICT solutions and having a clear vision can facilitate daily processes. (2) Adapting to the hyperconnectivity of the client (digital interconnection between persons and things at any place and time).	(1) Start collaborating digitally with commercial partners in a coordinated and efficient way.	(1) Continue to seek continuous improvement. As transformative, the company is very mature in terms of the exchange of digital information.

(continued)

Table 5.4 (continued)

Type of diagnosis knowledge of the industry 4.0	"Novice Company" Results (Basic level ICT) Actions	...level ICT Actions	"Transformative Company" (High level ICT) Actions
Operational processes Collaboration Skills development Client-centred culture Innovation	Attempt to accustom oneself to the use of ICTs as an established part of the organisation.	(1) Training employees in the use of ICTs can be help ease the transition (2) Helping employees become more experimental and active with ICTs. (3) Start adapting the portfolio of digital products and services.	(1) Focus constantly on the development of skills inherent in the exchange of digital information. (2) To propagate the exchange of digital information in an attempt to ensure other organisations become aware of the need. (3) Constantly update the portfolio of products and service to the digital world. (4) Promote and launch initiatives associated with applied research and the continued innovation in processes, products and services.

Source: Author's own

3.4 Digital Transformation Strategy Framework

The objective of the Digital Transformation strategy is to create the capacities necessary for taking maximum advantage of the possibilities and opportunities offered by new technologies and their impact in a more rapid, better and more innovative way in the future. A Digital Transformation journey needs a phase-based focus with a clear roadmap that involves a variety of interested parties, beyond the silos and limitations, internal and external. This Digital Transformation Strategy Framework takes into account the fact the final objectives will continue to advance given that digital technology is a continuous journey, just like digital change and innovation are.

In order to develop the Digital Transformation Strategy Framework, it is considered appropriate to have as a reference to (Harrison 2015) The Digital Strategy Guide. In Harrison´s Master Plan, the Digital Strategy consists of four main parts that which we will summarize and concretize according to the research approach proposed in the present work.

Phase 1: Insights and Analysis
Understanding the needs and priorities of the people who are at the core of your digital revolution including your customers, stakeholders, employees and executives. Analyze internal performance and sales data to understand where the biggest value is.

- External Digital Analysis
- Customer Experience Mapping
- Digital Value Chain Analysis

Phase 2: Digital Framework
Creating a framework that allows the company to addresses digital goals and objectives.

- The Iteration Model
- Big Idea / Mission / Vision
- Digital Objectives
- UVP

Phase 3: The Digital Scope
Addressing the company's approach to key areas of Digital and outlining the purpose, objectives and key initiatives and challenges of each channel.

- Website(s)
- Online Content
- Digital Advertising / SEM / SEO
- CRM
- Social
- Mobile
- ERP

Phase 4: Execution & Governance
Prioritizing the plan, taking into account, which needs are the most urgent and important as well as current resources, timelines and budgets. Digital business models become more agile we're forced to create plans that are iterative. Unlike traditional business planning, looking 3–5 years ahead is rarely realistic and accurate budgeting can be nearly impossible.

- Project priorities
- Project team(s)
- Accountability and Progress Reporting / KPI's

In substance, and in a broader sense, four main parts of the Digital Strategy are characterized by the following:

Phase 1: Insights & Analysis
Research is time-consuming and expensive, but it's nothing compared to the cost of a project that failed due to lack of diligence.

External Analysis (the Digital Way)
Since the Digital Strategy is about examining the business model as a whole, it is recommend starting with an external analysis like (Porter 2001) Porter's 5 Forces: threat of new entrants, determinants of supplier power, rivalry among existing firms, determinant of buyer power and threat of sustitutes. The exercise allows you to thoroughly consider and evaluate the digital threats and opportunities that could come from outside the business.

To keep the exercise focused, only analyze the 5 Forces as they relate to the digital business model.

A breakdown of how it works, as follows:

- Rivalry Among Existing Firms. To identify the threats and opportunities of direct competitors.
- Threat of New-Entrants. To think about the start-ups and companies that could become threats.
- Threat of Substitutes. To be on the lookout for new business models here.
- Determinants of Supplier Power. To consider what your suppliers are doing digitally but it could also mean that the power that your digital suppliers have over the company.
- Determinants of Buyer Power. To consider the power your digital buyer has and how the company can mitigate the risk involved in the customer relationship.

This factor is especially relevant to small to mid-size business units whose buyers are larger than they are.

Customer Experience Mapping
Designing your customer's experience starts with understanding and empathizing with their pain. Hopefully, you already have customer / user personas that represent your key targets. These personas shouldn't just be in a folder on your desktop—I recommend having them printed and on your wall so they're always top-of-mind.

Main aim: to use a Journey Mapping to outline the high-level experience of the customer lifecycle, then break it down into smaller pieces and layer in other components like sales activity, brand touch-points and user experience for the company website or app.

Journey mapping is an essential part of your Digital Strategy because it forces you to empathize with all of your users and stakeholders both internal and external. It also reduces confusion by making the process crystal clear.

Digital Value Chain Analysis
To do a traditional internal analysis of the value chain following Michael Porter's theory. Like the external analysis, we'll put a digital twist on it.

To keep in mind that this *does* apply to service businesses just as much as products. Language like "inbound logistics" suggests that we're only talking about a product business—but truthfully the process is just the same.

Starting with primary activities, take each business unit and break down its strengths and weaknesses.

- **Inbound Logistics**. To analyse the digital process of procuring goods from suppliers in the value-chain.
  To embrace dynamic ecosystems, in order to connect the company and suppliers together to rapidly and automatically respond to changing conditions.
  This digital ecosystem creates a dynamic supply chain, all the way from raw materials providers to end consumers, according to (Forrester 2016).
- To evaluate the digital aspects on the front-end of your value chain.
- **Operations**. To have an operations team happy with the software they are deaing with.
- **Outbound Logistics**. To evaluate the technology you use in your distribution processes. Extending products and services with digital technologies makes it possible to take greater mindshare within a customer's ecosystem of value, according to (Forrester 2016).
- **Marketing & Sales**. To focus on customer data as a big consideration. Taking into account that Marketing and Sales often need to leverage many online platforms for CRM, Content Management, E-Commerce, Business Intelligence, Lead Nurturing and much more. The Big Data movement is hitting these customer-facing units hard and the way you leverage company´s customer data should be regularly evaluated.
- **Service**. To focus on what happens after the purchase; the customer's service relationship with the brand long term and to provide them with what they need to be acdquired digitally.

Phase 2: Digital Framework
Main aim: to create a framework that allows the company to addresses digital goals and objectives. To cast an overall vision for what digital will be doing for the company. This includes one big idea and your digital objectives.

Create Your Iteration Model

To consider the Digital Transformation as an evolutionary process — not a traditional business plan where we plan then execute over long periods of time. In fact, most digital work should happen in 6-week sprints where company should be focusing all the energy on one important short-term goal.

Distilled to One Big Idea

Since your Digital Strategy is all about people, you *need* people to believe in your ideas and adopt them as their own. To distill the entire plan to one big idea that everyone can remember and believe in.

Examples:
We are...

- Turning visitors into customers
- Going from "great" to "irreplaceable"
- Becoming our customers' favorite company

To circle back to this exercise at the end of your process.

Digital Base

Your Goals and Objectives. To define what the digital program to do for the company. To describe both the goal and the objectives that will be used to complete it.

Here are some definitions for the purpose of this exercise:

Digital Goal: This crystallizes the thing that stakeholders want most.

Example:

Goal 1: To increase mobility for national sales force and account managers, giving them visibility into the sales pipeline, account activity and company performance.

4   OBJECTIVES:

To seek and implement a CRM platform that is accompanied by a mobile app to capture and view lead data on the road

To find or create a mobile tablet app for account managers that gives mobile visibility to current account data in our inventory management and payment processing systems.

4.1   Digital Scope: To Address the Company's Approach to Key Areas of Digital and Outline the Purpose, Key Initiatives and Challenges of Each Objective

This is where things start to get a little hairy (and potentially exhausting for some audiences). In company's digital scope, to take a deeper look at each objective which is outlined in company's Digital Base.

To put in company's Digital Scope, taking into account some insights on the most common objectives and channels, such as:

(a) **Website(s)**. To have a branded websites as it is a huge factor in buyers' buying decisions.

(b) **Online Content**. Blogging should be done strategically to produce astounding results like more leads, larger email lists, and better search traffic.

(c) **Digital Advertising / SEM / SEO**. To target very specific users and the links actually go straight to the app store. As Facebook and Google have ad programs specifically designed for mobile apps and potential customer are looking for;
  - credible sources
  - recommended by others
  - informative
  - relevant
  - visually educational
  - organized
  - appropriate
  - accompanied by a good user experience
  - To create blog posts and web pages that accomplishes these things.

(d) **Customer Relationship Management (CRM)**. To customize the CRM use and to use the journey mapping example above by mapping out the entire sales process to ensure that the leveraging of CRM to the max.

(e) **Social**. To understand what role social business plays in your organization and sales funnel. The new path to success in Social is to integrate social into your other channels and customer experiences—both online and offline.

To create opportunities for company's customers to share.

4.2   Execution & Governance

Main aim: To prioritize the plan, taking into account which needs are the most urgent and important as well as current resources, timelines and budgets.

Prioritizing Your Projects
To have lazar-like focus on just a handful of projects (usually 3–5) instead of overwhelming yourself with all of them.

To decide which projects go first, consider the impact each initiative will have on the following factors:

– Bottom-line
– Employee morale
– Productivity
– Brand Equity
– Customer Experience

To choose the handful of projects that will make the biggest impact and commit the time, money and resources to get it done.

Iterative Governance Models
To decide on a framework for how your digital project teams should function toward the end of the strategy phase. To empower the teams in order to make critical decisions as a high-functioning business unit, not a traditional department silo.

Finally, in summary, the way forward would be (Fig. 5.8);

4.3   Digital Transformation Strategy Development Plan

As observed in previous sections, all aspects (hereinafter the connecting elements) mentioned are connected, they superimpose on one other and not all are directly related to redefining and/or creating new technology models. Although it is true that the main strategic focus is on the business;

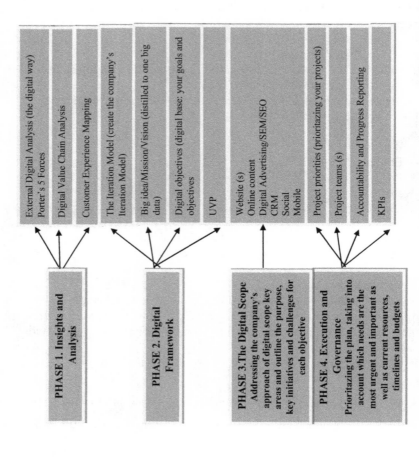

Fig. 5.8 Digital transformation strategy framework (phases and actions/activities' interrelation). (Source: Author's own)

the definition of the Digital Strategy constitutes a comprehensive vision of Digital Transformation through which aspects such as customer experience, the evolution of technologies and innovation play a key role. But for the evolution of the development plan for the strategy, we must be aware that other elements interact and cannot be ignored.

The objective of the Digital Transformation strategy is to create the capacities necessary for taking maximum advantage of the possibilities and opportunities offered by new technologies and their impact in a more rapid, better and more innovative way in the future.[3] A Digital Transformation journey needs a phase-based focus with a clear roadmap that involves a variety of interested parties, beyond the silos and limitations, internal and external. This roadmap (development plan) takes into account the fact the final objectives will continue to advance given that digital technology is a continuous journey, just like digital change and innovation are.

Digital Strategy Plan Design
A Digital Strategy or plan is the articulation of an organisation's vision, goals and purpose for engaging with digital solutions and technologies. It articulates the opportunities and challenges related to digital activities, the governance and management arrangements and risk management issues. It lays out a plan of action in order to maximise the business benefits of digital initiatives to the organisation.

The connecting elements of the phases of development associated with the design of the development plan of the Digital Strategy will include those presented graphically below (Table 5.5).

4.4   *Digital Transformation Strategy's Balance Scorecard*

While some models of organizational effectiveness go in and out of fashion, one that has persisted is the McKinsey 7-S framework. Developed in the early 1980s by Tom Peters and Robert Waterman, two consultants working at the McKinsey & Company consulting firm, the basic premise

---

[3] Definition available from https://www.i-scoop.eu/digital-transformation/.

Table 5.5 The design of the digital transformation strategy development plan phases

Phase 1	**Analyse the external environment** (according to type of industry)	Adaptation to digital strategic framework	– Channel strategy – Assessment of opportunity	
	Analyse the internal environment **The client value chain**	Definition of level of digital maturity and diagnosis	Governance	
Phase 2	**Define the business model**	– Assessment scorecard – Definition of Digital Strategy		
Phase 3	**Define and analyse the target market**	Phase 1 (analysis of external environment)	Type of industry	Specific characteristics of Industry 4.0 framework
Phase 4	**Review and optimise**	Business and commercial process management		
		Business and automation processes	Adaptation to digital strategic framework	Operational processes
Phase 5	**Improve the client experience**	Adaptation to digital strategic framework (client 360)		– Client knowledge – Client journey – Governance – "Active" listening
Phase 6	**Foster a new organisational culture**	Adaptation to digital strategic framework	Operational processes	– Globalisation – Skills development – Client focussed culture – Innovation
Phase 7	**Adopt the most appropriate technological solutions and perform continued benchmarking actions**	Adaptation to digital strategic framework	Technology and data	Governance
Phase 8	**Know the new business ecosystems**			
Phase 9	**Develop scorecards based on analytics to assess Digital Strategy**			

Source: Author's own

of the model is that there are seven internal aspects of an organization that need to be aligned if it is to be successful.

The 7-S model can be used in a wide variety of situations where an alignment perspective is useful, for example, to help you:

- Improve the performance of a company.
- Examine the likely effects of future changes within a company.
- Align departments and processes during a merger or acquisition.
- Determine how best to implement a proposed strategy.

The McKinsey 7-S model can be applied to elements of a team or a project as well. The alignment issues apply, regardless of how you decide to define the scope of the areas you study. How you can align them to improve performance in your organization.

4.5   The Seven Elements

The McKinsey 7-S model involves seven interdependent factors, which are categorized as either "hard" or "soft" elements (Table 5.6):

"Hard" elements are easier to define or identify and management can directly influence them: These are strategy statements; organisation charts and reporting lines; and formal processes and IT systems.

"Soft" elements, on the other hand, can be more difficult to describe, and are less tangible and more influenced by culture. However, these soft elements are as important as the hard elements if the organisation is going to be successful.

Table 5.6   Mckinsey 7-S model' seven elements

Hard elements	Soft elements
Strategy	Shared Values
Structure	Skills
Systems	Style
	Staff

Source: McKinsey 7-S Model

The way the model is presented in Table 5.6 below depicts the interdependency of the elements and indicates how a change in one affects all the others.

Let's look at each of the elements specifically:

- **Strategy**: the plan devised to maintain and build competitive advantage over the competition.
- **Structure**: the way the organization is structured and who reports to whom.
- **Systems**: the daily activities and procedures that staff members engage in to get the job done.
- **Shared Values**: called "superordinate goals" when the model was first developed, these are the core values of the company that are evidenced in the corporate culture and the general work ethic.
- **Style**: the style of leadership adopted.
- **Staff**: the employees and their general capabilities.
- **Skills**: the actual skills and competencies of the employees working for the company.

MCKinsey 7-S scorecard worksheets for developing "Phase 4 Accountability and Progress reporting and KPIs" linked to Digital Strategy development plan phases and actions of Strategic Digital Transformation Plan "Phase 9 Develop scorecards based on analytics to assess Digital Strategy") (Tables 5.7 and 5.8).

Current Situation (Point A) Digital Strategy Implementation Plan
Future Situation (Point B) Digital Strategy Implementation Plan (KPIs integrated)

- "Phase 4 Accountability and Progress reporting and KPIs"Assess the company's progress in digitazing its current business models.
- Assess new revenue sources generated from new digital business models.

Table 5.7 Current situation (Mckinsey 7-S model scorecard-point A)

	Shared Values	Strategy	Structure	Systems	Style	Staff	Skills
Shared values	Phase I Analyse the internal environment						
Strategy		Phase I Adaptation to digital strategic framework					
Structure			Phase I Governance				
Systems				Phase 4 Business and commercial process management Business and automation processes Operational processes			
Style					Phase 7 Governance		
Staff						Phase 6 Foster a new organisational culture	
Skills							Phase 6 Skills development

Source: Author's own

Table 5.8 Future situation (Mckinsey 7-S model scorecard-point B)

	Shared values	Strategy FINANCIAL IMPACT (Digital Transformation metric)	Structure OPERATIONAL IMPROVEMENT (Digital Transformation metric)	Systems OPERATIONAL IMPROVEMENT & CUSTOMER EXPERIENCE (Digital Transformation metrics)	Style	Staff	Skills
Shared values		Measure the overall progress of the Digital Transformation plan Using specific reference to the value of each digital initiative	Assess and quantify the benefits of each digital initiative				
Strategy		Time and costs savings Revenue Growth percentage Measuring goals in products/services					
Structure			Web assets or new digital product				
Systems							
Style				Customer engagement Retention rates Market shares Measuring goals in sales, marketing, operations, supply chain and customer services			
Staff			Measuring impact in terms of work climate derived from the change		Employee engagement		
Skills				Measuring impact of internal training plan			

Source: Author's own

REFERENCES

Adams, R., Bessant, J., & Phelps, R. (2006). Innovation Management Measurement: A Review. *International Journal of Management Reviews, 8*(1), 21–47. Retrieved November 5, 2016, from http://oapen.org/search?identifier=560292.

Chesbrough, H., & Rosenbloom, S. R. (2002). The Role of the Business Model in Capturing Value from Innovation: Evidence from Xerox Corporation's Technology Spin-Offs Companies. *Industrial and Corporate Change, 11*(3), 529–555.

Connect and Construct. (2014). *Digital Maturity Assessment.* Retrieved January 19, 2018, from http://www.connectandconstruct.eu/microsite/digital_maturity.php.

Descartes, R. (1983). *Principles of Philosophy,* trans. V.R. Miller and R.P. Miller.

Engel, C. (1999). The Internet and the Nation State. *Lectiones Jenenses, 21.*

Forrester. (2016). *The Digital Maturity Model 4.0.* Retrieved March 4, 2018, from https://forrester.nitro-digital.com/pdf/Forrester-s%20Digital%20Maturity%20Model%204.0.pdf.

Harmancioglu, N., Droge, C., & Calantone, R. J. (2009). Strategic Fit to Resources Versus NPD Execution Proficiencies: What are their Roles in Determining Success? *Journal of the Academy of Marketing Science, 37*(3), 266–282.

Harrison, J. (2015). *The Digital Strategy Guide.* Retrieved August 2018, from http://www.harrisonjlloyd.com/2015/03/30/the-digital-strategy-guide-i-couldnt-find-with-examples-and-templates/#structure.

Holmstro, J., & Nyle, D. (2015). Digital Innovation Strategy: A Framework for Diagnosing and Improving Digital Product and Service Innovation. *Business Horizons, 58*(1), 57–67.

Porter, M. E. (2001). Strategy and the Internet. *Harvard Business Review, 79*(2), 62–78.

Powell, T. (1992). Organizational Alignment as Competitive Advantage. *Strategic Management Journal, 13,* 119–134.

Succar, B. (2009). Building Information Modelling Framework: A Research and Delivery Foundation for Industry Stakeholders. *Automation in Construction, 18*(3), 357–375. Retrieved March 15, 2018, from https://www.academia.edu/170356/Building_Information_Modelling_framework_a_research_and_delivery_foundation_for_industry_stakeholders.

CONCLUSIONS

This book makes significant progress in our understanding of the strategic Digital Transformation framework use within the Industry 4.0 and current Digital Transformation overall context for companies to ensure their current and future competitive advantage in the market, regardless of the sector in which they develop their activity.

This book presents as its main contribution the construction of a Strategic Digital Transformation operational framework, necessary and adaptable to any type of company and sector of activity.

The main purpose of this work was to define a simplified and integrated model of various tools and actions to allow for the integration of companies in the Industry 4.0 ecosystem. Over the course of the study, certain temporal and economic limitations were encountered which have impeded the technological development of the most complete tools (e.g., the type actions: integration of a scorecard based on analytics for assessment of the Digital Strategy in accordance with the training plan inherent in the new digital-professional competency context, the generation of a strategic business case adapted to the digital context and the generation of a benchmarking map allowing for analysis of the external context of the emerging technologies adapted according to the sector of activity of the company with respect to Industry 4.0).

While we have generated a number of new and redesign patterns, actions, approaches and several measures, useful tools, given the in-depth sampling strategy focused on exploring the literature and, very little can be

A. Landeta Echeberria, *A Digital Framework for Industry 4.0*, https://doi.org/10.1007/978-3-030-60049-5

said of the nature of Digital Transformation strategy for increasing businesses' competitiveness nowadays.

Further, Digital Transformations are often accompanied by changing skill sets that are not only necessary for the transformation itself, but also for regular operations thereafter. While current staff members may have a different, less tech-savvy mindset and may lack the required technological capabilities to cope with the upcoming changes, new highly skilled and focused staff members might be difficult to find, given the particular location of a firm. Research could support firms by providing guidance on the assessment of their existing technological capabilities and on procedures to weigh up their current options, as well as guidance on the design of training procedures for current employees and new hires.

This calls for concrete recommendations for procedures for the continuous refinement of Digital Transformation strategies, such as how to observe and evaluate technological developments and how to test their impacts in controlled environments within the company. Other key questions include the desired extent of Digital Transformation

Integrating Digital Transformation Strategies into Firms

As noted, Digital Transformation strategies have a cross-functional character and need to be aligned with other functional and operational strategies. However, the alignment of IT strategies with other strategies has remained a difficult and controversial endeavor. Given the rather recent appearance of Digital Transformation strategies, further evidence is needed as to how this alignment can be conducted in practice—not only related to IT strategies, but also from an organisational perspective. In this respect, the interaction of Digital Transformation strategies with business development and business models also needs to be assessed from a management perspective. Since Digital Transformation strategies cut across various other strategies at the same time, complex coordination efforts might be needed. Research should provide guidelines for firms to help structure these processes in order to achieve shared goal setting, the alignment of different strategies, and cooperation between various people and entities throughout a firm.

Therefore, to resolve several theoretical and methodological issues will be required.

The first issue is the need for adopting exponential technology functions such as

- Favour corporate entrepreneurship: offering companies good opportunities to invest in new trends at an early stage and to benefit from disruptive innovation and exponential technologies.
- Foster the generation of learning organisations: companies must become learning organisations if they want to take full advantage of exponential technologies to achieve Digital Transformation (Industry 4.0).
- Improve efficiency in the management of innovation: the successful management of innovation covers the entire company and the strategy, the organisation and administration of the portfolio of products and product development. The Digital Transformation of Industry 4.0 allows for us to even further improve the efficiency of innovation management in all these areas.
- Generate an interactive and adapted curriculum: this will make individual learning possible, thus accelerating strategic implementation and organisational development.
- Adopt the most appropriate technological solutions and carry out continuous benchmarking actions when faced with changing behaviour and the constant emergence of new technologies associated with the business ecosystem of Industry 4.0.

The second issue is associated with skill requirements in the digital world and talent development practices for Industry 4.0:

- Foster the generation of learning organisations: companies must become learning organisations if they want to take full advantage of current and emerging technologies to achieve Digital Transformation (Industry 4.0).
- Design an interactive curriculum adapted to the company's strategic plan: this will facilitate individual learning and the design of ad hoc training activities.
- Adopt more appropriate technological solutions and carry out continuous internal training activities when faced with changing behaviour and the constant emergence of new technologies associated with the business ecosystem of Industry 4.0.

- Consider the evolution-transformation of the labour market; the reinvention arising from future typology of the workforce, emerging digital professions and new forms of work.
- Assess the impact on productivity and the commitment of employees. Analysing the different combinations of the digitalisation of the workplace and the workforce, with the entry of a broad group of new internal departments or functional units and/or the adaptation of it to ICTs, including (but are not limited to R&D&I) the pairing of Senior Management and Human Resources.

Accordingly, the principal conclusions drawn in entrepreneurial and technological terms are the following:

IN BUSINESS TERMS

The development of a digital culture is one of the key pillars of the Digital Transformation of companies. The Digital Transformation requires new behaviours on the part of directors and managers to lead the transformation and ensure that full advantage is taken of digital technologies and platforms.

The Digital Transformation and the process require perfect alignment with the company's strategy throughout the different levels of maturity.

The Digital Transformation requires an interdisciplinary and multidimensional model that redefines the bases and premises upon which the organisation competes and meets and satisfies the needs of their customers, interrelates with partners in organisational ecosystems and generates income and profit for shareholders and/or investors.

The need for greater involvement on the part of the general management in SMEs who must tackle the challenge from three perspectives: the individual/organisational, the functional and the industrial.

At the individual level, the technological capacity of employees to adopt digital resources is necessary. Moreover, they must ensure that the organisation has resources that support Digital Transformation. In this sense, management must integrate and communicate a clear digital vision to the entire organisation.

The organisation must provide its employees with some directives on how to use resources to take full advantage of digital technologies. Ultimately, the general management of SMEs must employ competent workers with the right skills to help the company in its Digital Transformation.

At the industrial level, the general management of SMEs must pay attention to emerging trends and technologies to quickly identify the right opportunities for their organisation.

Managers must be conscious of these changes and capable of acting ahead so as not to be left behind by competitors. Consequently, it is essential that every manager ensure that their division understands that adapting to the Digital Transformation is a business project and not an information technology project.

In Technological Terms

The existence of emerging technologies must lead to detailed analysis of their foreseen application: the models of digital maturity are emerging as an integrated framework that allows organisation to evolve progressively in the development of capacities to be successful in the new digital era.

The maturity models show capacities relevant to all sectors and, in some cases, provide specific capacity for certain sectors.

Finally, it is imperative that practioners understand how this important resource best be used within the complex contextual relationships within the firm. It is important that relationships that affect the success of strategic Digital Transformation framework planning be studied and the results presented for increasing the understanding of both executives and researchers. This book has attempted to add and extend the body of knowledge surrounding strategic Digital Transformation ecosystems (business, research and innovation). It lays the groundwork for both practice and future research.

At the close of this edition, we cannot neglect to mention the Covid-19 pandemic. The themes of the book are perhaps more relevant now than ever, with the digitalisation of the business fabric becoming an imperative as the Covid-19 crisis has forced many businesses to accelerate their digitalisation plans.

The pandemic has disrupted the business model and operations of many companies and institutions, requiring constant innovation and the ability to anticipate in a context of uncertainty.

A key aspect of the transformation has been increased digitalisation and the accelerated implementation of existing trends such as Online Shopping and Robot Deliveries, Digital and Contactless Payments, Remote Work,

Distance Learning, Telehealth, Online Entertainment, Supply Chain 4.0, 3D Printing, Robotics and Drones and 5G and Information and Communications Technology.

The Covid-19 crisis is therefore likely to significantly accelerate the shift to digital and fundamentally alter the business landscape. Staying current in the latest technology will be essential for any business looking to remain competitive in a post-Covid-19 world.

INDEX

CPSIA information can be obtained
at www.ICGtesting.com
Printed in the USA
LVHW021044220321
682067LV00001B/25